HBR Guide to
Persuasive Presentations

Harvard Business Review Guides

Arm yourself with the advice you need to succeed on the job, from the most trusted brand in business. Packed with how-to essentials from leading experts, the HBR Guides provide smart answers to your most pressing work challenges.

The titles include:

HBR Guide to Better Business Writing

HBR Guide to Finance Basics for Managers

HBR Guide to Getting the Mentoring You Need

HBR Guide to Getting the Right Job

HBR Guide to Getting the Right Work Done

HBR Guide to Giving Effective Feedback

HBR Guide to Making Every Meeting Matter

HBR Guide to Managing Stress

HBR Guide to Managing Up and Across

HBR Guide to Persuasive Presentations

HBR Guide to Project Management

HBR Guide to
Persuasive
Presentations

Nancy Duarte

HARVARD BUSINESS REVIEW PRESS

Boston, Massachusetts

Library of Congress Cataloging-in-Publication Data

Duarte, Nancy.
   HBR guide to persuasive presentations / Nancy Duarte.
      p. cm.
   ISBN 978-1-4221-8710-4 (alk. paper)
   1. Business presentations.   2. Persuasion (Psychology)   I. Title.
   HF5718.22.D817 2012
   658.4′52—dc23

                                              2012019634

The paper used in this publication meets the requirements of the American National Standard for Permanence of Paper for Publications and Documents in Libraries and Archives Z39.48–1992.

What You'll Learn

Do you dread giving presentations? Maybe your mind goes blank when you sit down to generate ideas, or you struggle to organize your fragmented thoughts and data into a coherent, persuasive message. Is it tough to connect with customers you're wooing, senior executives you're hitting up for funding, or employees you're training? Do you fumble for the right words, get lost in your slide deck, run out of time before you've hit your main points—and leave the room uncertain you've gotten through to *anyone*?

This guide will give you the confidence and tools you need to engage your audience, sell your ideas, and inspire people to act. You'll get better at:

- Showing people why your ideas matter to *them*

- Winning over tough crowds

- Balancing analytical and emotional appeal

- Crafting memorable messages

- Creating powerful visuals

What You'll Learn

- Striking the right tone

- Holding your audience's attention

- Measuring your impact

Contents

Section 4: MEDIA
Identify the best modes for communicating your message.

Section 5: SLIDES
Conceptualize and simplify the display of information.

Section 6: DELIVERY
Deliver your presentation authentically.

Contents

Section 7: IMPACT
Measure—and increase—your presentation's impact on your audience.

Introduction

If I am to speak for ten minutes, I need a week for
preparation; if fifteen minutes, three days; if half
an hour, two days; if an hour, I am ready now.

—**Woodrow T. Wilson**

We work in a first-draft culture. Type an e-mail. Send.
Write a blog entry. Post. Whip up some slides. Speak.

But it's in crafting and recrafting—in iteration and rehearsal—that excellence emerges.

Why worry about being an excellent communicator
when you have so many other pressing things to do? Because it will help you *get those things done.*

So as you conceive, visualize, and present your message, don't skimp on preparation, even if you're giving
a short talk. It actually takes more careful planning to
distill your ideas into a few key takeaways than it does
to create an hour-long presentation (see figure I-1). And
gather lots of feedback so you'll be all the more effective
when you start the process again.

FIGURE I-1

Planning a presentation

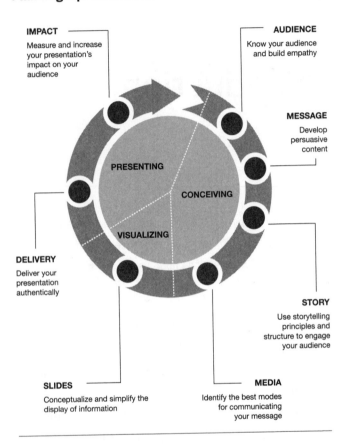

Since 1990, I've run a firm that specializes in writing and producing presentations—and then I became a presenter myself. This book is loaded with insights learned from supporting other presenters and giving my own talks. But, trust me, I've had my share of embarrassing moments, many of which could have been avoided with a little planning. Loading the wrong presentation onto my laptop. Walking onstage with my skirt tucked into my underwear. Botching my delivery to executives at an $8 billion company because I hadn't rehearsed enough—and getting cut from their continuing series of meetings. Experience is a powerful teacher.

I've also learned a lot from success. When audiences can see that you've prepared—that you care about their needs and value their time—they'll want to connect with you and support you. You'll get people to adopt your ideas, and you'll win the resources to carry them out. You'll close more deals. You'll earn the backing of decision makers. You'll gain influence. In short, you'll go farther in your organization—and your career.

Special thanks to:

- The wonderful Lisa Burrell, who edited my mess into coherence

- The entire team at Duarte, who supported me with case studies

- Members of the Twitterverse who answered my questions: @annzerega, @caddguru, @carolmquig, @catiehargrove, @charlesgreene3, @ckallaos, @conniewinch, @iamanshul, @karlparry, @managebetternow, @matthewmccull, @moniquemaley, @mpacc, @speakingtall, and @zupermik

Section 1
Audience

Designing a presentation without an audience in mind is like writing a love letter and addressing it "to whom it may concern."

—**Ken Haemer,**
  Presentation Research Manager, AT&T

Understand the Audience's Power

When you walk into a room as a presenter, it's easy to feel as if you're in a position of power: You're up front, perhaps even elevated on a stage, and people came to hear you speak. In reality, though, you're not the star of the show. The audience is.

Why? The people you're addressing will determine whether your idea spreads or dies, simply by embracing or rejecting it. You need them more than they need you. Since they have that control, it's crucial to be humble in your approach. Use their desires and goals as a filter for everything you present.

Presenters tend to be self-focused. They have a lot to say, they want to say it well, and they have little time to prepare. These pressures make them forget what's important to the audience. A self-focused presenter might just describe a new initiative and explain what needs to get done—outlining how to do it, when to do it, and the budget required. Then maybe, if the audience is lucky, he'll have a slide at the very end about "why it matters."

This format screams, "I pay you to do this, so just do it!" The presenter is so consumed by the mission that he forgets to say why people would want or need to be involved.

Spend a moment in your audience's shoes. Walk people through why the initiative matters to them and to the organization, what internal and external factors are driving it, and why their support will make it successful. Yes, get through the nitty-gritty details, but set up the valuable role they'll play in the scenario rather than dictate a laundry list of to-do's.

Though presentations and audiences vary, one important fact remains constant: The people in your audience came to see what you can do for them, not what they must do for you. So look at the audience as the "hero" of your idea—and yourself as the mentor who helps people see themselves in that role so they'll want to get behind your idea and propel it forward.

Think of Yoda—a classic example of a wise, humble mentor. In the *Star Wars* movies, he gives the hero, Luke Skywalker, a special gift (a deeper understanding of the "Force"), trains him to use a magical tool (the lightsaber), and helps him in his fight against the Empire.

Like Yoda and other mentors in mythology, presenters should:

- **Give the hero a special gift:** Give people insights that will improve their lives. Perhaps you introduce senior managers at your company to an exciting new way to compete in the marketplace. Or maybe you show a roomful of potential clients that you can save them money and time.

- **Teach the hero to use a "magical" tool:** This is where the people in your audience pick up a new skill or mind-set from you—something that enables them to reach their objectives *and* yours.

- **Help the hero get "unstuck":** Ideally, you'll come with an idea or a solution that gets the audience out of a difficult or painful situation.

So if you're gearing up to launch a new service offering, for example, give your team a clear roadmap (tool) and a promise to bring in consultants for training and support (gift)—and describe how these will help everyone rise to the challenge ahead.

Segment the Audience

If you see your audience as a homogenous, faceless clump of people, you'll have a hard time making a connection and moving them to action. Instead, think of them as a line of individuals waiting to have a conversation with you.

Your audience will usually include a mix of people—individuals in diverse roles, with various levels of decision-making authority, from different parts of the organization—each needing to hear your message for different reasons. Decide which subgroup is the most important to you, and zero in on that subgroup's needs when you develop your presentation.

When you're segmenting your audience, take a look at:

- **Politics:** Power, influence, decision process

- **Demographics:** Age, education, ethnicity, gender, and geography

- **Psychographics:** Personality, values, attitudes, interests, communities, and lifestyle

- **Firmographics:** Number of employees, revenue size, industry, number of locations, location of headquarters

- **Ethnographics:** Social and cultural needs

After you've segmented the group, figure out which members will have the greatest impact on the adoption of your idea. Is there a layer of management you need to appeal to? Is there a type of customer in the room with a lot of sway over the industry?

Then view yourself as a curator of content for your most valuable and powerful stakeholders. Pick the one type of person in the room with the most influence, and write your presentation as if just to that subgroup. The presentation can't be so specialized that it will alienate everyone else—you'll need some content that appeals to the greater group. But tailor most of your specifics to the subgroup you've targeted.

Say you're presenting a new product concept to the executive team, and you know you won't get their buy-in unless Trent, the president of the enterprise division, gets excited about the idea, because they always defer to his instincts on new initiatives. Appeal first to Trent's entrepreneurial nature by describing how exciting the new market is—while keeping in mind what the other executives will care about. Here's where your segmentation work will come in handy (table 1-1).

Draw on your understanding of the team members as you prepare your talk. In addition to fanning the flames of Trent's entrepreneurism, for example, have data in your pocket to respond to Marco, the analytical and

TABLE 1-1

Segmenting your audience

Executive team member	Qualities
Bert, CEO	Hierarchical, micromanager, dominant, fear-driven, needs to be liked
Carol, president of Consumer division	Visionary, creative, disruptive, scattered, wants to stand on own feet
Trent, president of Enterprise division	Entrepreneurial, design thinker, systematic, found self after near-death experience
Martin, CMO	CEO's favorite, empirically minded, arrogant, sabotages projects
Marco, CTO	Political, risk-averse, analytical, introverted, has self-doubt

risk-averse CTO, when he inevitably balks. And try to work with, not against, your CMO's arrogance: Ask for his counsel on a key marketing point or two before the group meets, and he'll be less likely to lash out during the presentation or sit there quietly plotting a coup, as is his wont.

What if some audience members are already familiar with your idea and others need to be brought up to speed? (This is most likely to happen when you're presenting within your organization.) Consider evening things out by giving the newbies a crash course before you conduct the larger presentation. Or you may decide just to do two separate presentations.

Present Clearly and Concisely to Senior Executives

Senior executives are a tough segment to reach. They usually have very little time in their schedules to give you. Though that's true of many audiences, what sets this crowd apart is that they need to make huge decisions based on accurate information delivered quickly. Long presentations with a big reveal at the end do not work for them. They'll want you to get to the bottom line right away—and they often won't let you finish your shtick without interrupting. (Never mind that you would have answered their questions if they'd just let you get through the next three slides.)

When presenting to an audience of senior executives, do everything you can to make their decision making easier and more efficient:

- **Get to the point:** Take less time than you were allocated. If you were given 30 minutes, create your talk within that timeframe but then pretend that your slot got cut to 5 minutes. That'll force you to be succinct and lead with the things they care about—high-level findings, conclusions, recommendations, your call to action. Hit those points clearly and simply before you venture into supporting data or tangential areas of importance to you.

- **Give them what they asked for:** Stay on topic. If you were invited to give an update about the flooding of the manufacturing plant in Indonesia, do that before covering anything else. They've invited you because they felt you could supply a missing piece of information, so answer that specific request quickly.

- **Set expectations:** At the beginning, let the audience know you will spend the first 5 of your 30 minutes presenting your summary and the remaining time on discussion. Most executives will be patient for 5 minutes and let you present your main points well if they know they'll be able to ask questions fairly soon.

- **Create executive summary slides:** Develop a clear, short overview of your key points, and place it in a set of executive summary slides at the front of the deck; have the rest of your slides serve as an appendix. Follow a 10% rule of thumb: If your appendix is 50 slides, devote about 5 slides to your summary at the beginning. After you present the summary, let the group drive the conversation.

Often, executives will want to go deeper on the points that will aid their decision making. You can quickly pull up any slides in the appendix that speak to those points.

- **Rehearse:** Before presenting, run your slides by someone who has success getting ideas adopted at the executive level and who will serve as an honest coach. Is your message coming through clearly and quickly? Do your summary slides boil everything down into skimmable key insights? Are you missing anything your audience is likely to expect?

Sounds like a lot of work, right? It is, but presenting to an executive team is a great honor and can open tremendous doors. If you nail this, people with a lot of influence will become strong advocates for your ideas.

Get to Know Your Audience

Segmenting your audience members politically, demographically, psychographically, and so on is a great start, but connecting with people means understanding them on a more personal level. To develop resonant content for them, dig for deeper insights about them. Ask yourself:

- **What are they like?** Think through a day in their lives. Describe what that looks like so they'll know you "get" them.

- **Why are they here?** What do they think they're going to get out of this presentation? Are they willing participants or mandatory attendees? Highlight what's in it for them.

- **What keeps them up at night?** Everyone has a fear, a pain point, a thorn in the side. Let your audience know that you empathize—and that you're here to help.

- **How can you solve their problems?** How are you going to make their lives better? Point to benefits you know they'll care about.

- **What do you want them to do?** What's their part in your plan? Make sure there's a clear action for your audience to take. (See "Build an Effective Call to Action" in the Message section of this guide.)

- **How might they resist?** What will keep them from adopting your message and carrying out your call to action? Remove any obstacles you can.

- **How can you best reach them?** How do they prefer to receive information? Do they like the room to be set up a certain way? Do they want materials to review before the presentation? Afterward? What atmosphere or type of media will best help them see your point of view? Give them what they want, how they want it.

When getting ready to present to an audience you've never met, do some research online. If you know the names of stakeholders in your audience, look up their bios. If you know only generalities about the audience, find the event on social media feeds and read what's on the minds of those who'll be attending. If you'll be presenting to a company, find recent press mentions, look at how the company positions itself against competitors, read its annual report, and have Google Alerts send new articles about the company to your e-mail.

One time, I was preparing to present to beer executives, and I don't like beer or know anything about the industry. So I hosted a beer-tasting event at my shop, read their annual report, read recent press, studied key influencers, and looked up each attendee online. During the Q&A, a question came from one of the top executives (I knew he was at the top because I'd looked him up)— and I answered his question with timely examples.

When your audience is familiar—say, a group of your direct reports or colleagues—think through the pressures they are under and find ways to create an empathic connection.

Knowing people—*really* knowing them—makes it easier to influence them. You engage in a conversation, exchange insights, tell stories. Usually, both you and they change a bit in the process.

People don't fall asleep during conversations, but they often do during presentations—and that's because many presentations don't *feel conversational*. Knowing your audience well helps you feel warmly toward the people in the room and take on a more conversational tone. Speak sincerely to your audience, and people will want to listen to your message and root for and contribute to the success of your idea.

Define How You'll Change the Audience

When you present, you're asking the people in the room to change their behavior or beliefs in some way, big or small. Before you begin writing your presentation, map out that transformation—where your audience is starting, and where you want people to end up. This is the most critical step in planning your presentation, because that desired endpoint is the whole reason you're presenting in the first place, and people won't get there on their own.

Ask yourself, "What new beliefs do I want them to adopt? How do I want them to behave differently? How must their attitudes or emotions change before their behavior can change?"

By thinking through who they are before they enter the room and who you want them to be when they leave, you'll define their transformation arc, much as a screenwriter plans the protagonist's transformation in a film.

Let's say you work in the development office at a university and you're delivering a presentation to potential donors. The audience transformation might look like the one shown in table 1-2.

TABLE 1-2

Transforming your audience

Move audience from:	Move audience to:
Skepticism that the school will make good use of the money	Excitement about innovative research by faculty, students, and alumni—and an impulse to give

Change typically doesn't happen without a struggle. It's hard to convince people to move away from a view that is comfortable or widely held as true, or change a behavioral pattern that has become their norm. You are persuading members of your audience to let go of old beliefs or habits and adopt new ones. Once you understand their transformation, you can demonstrate empathy for the sacrifices they may need to make to move your idea forward.

Find Common Ground

Whether you evoke frenzied enthusiasm or puzzled stares or glassy-eyed boredom depends largely on how well your message resonates with the audience.

Resonance is a physics phenomenon. If you tap into an object's natural rate of vibration, or *resonant frequency*, it will move: It may vibrate, shudder, or even play a sympathetic musical note—think tuning forks. The same is true, metaphorically, when you present to an audience. If you tap into the group's resonant frequency, you can *move* the people listening to you.

But how do you resonate deeply enough to move them toward your objective? Figure out where you have common ground, and communicate on that frequency. Think about what's inside them that's also inside you. That way, you're not pushing or pulling them; they're moving because you tapped into something they already believe.

All this may sound highly unscientific and touchy-feely, but you can find your audience's resonant frequency by doing a little research. You'll want to examine:

- **Shared experiences:** What from your past do you have in common. Do you share memories, historical events, interests?

- **Common goals:** Where are you all headed in the future? What types of outcomes are mutually desired?

- **Qualifications:** Why are you uniquely qualified to be the audience's guiding expert? What did you learn when you faced similar challenges of your own, and how will your audience benefit from that insight?

The amount of common ground you discover will depend on the depth of your relationship with the group.

Lots of common ground

If you are presenting to family, friends, club members, or a religous group, it's easy to find common ground because you know the people well and tend to share many experiences, interests, and values.

Moderate common ground

With your colleagues, the challenge is a bit tougher. You know them a bit, but not as much as close friends or relatives. You share some interests but possibly only around one or two things. Examine those points of intersection for a way in.

Let's say you're a scientist working for a biotech company and you've been asked to speak at an all-hands meeting. Most of the audience members will be scientists, but you'll also be addressing executives and administrative employees. To find common ground with them, think about why you decided to work for this company and what motivates you to do your job day to day. Maybe you wanted to use your research and problem-solving skills to help people stay healthy—a mission the others in the room will share or at least support. Finding such commonalities will help you connect with them.

Minimal common ground

With a broad audience—for instance, a group of seminar participants from a variety of organizations and industries—you'll have many types of people to think about. The overlap won't be immediately evident, because there are so many perspectives and backgrounds to consider. You'll need to work hard to find or create it, but that work will pay off.

Before I went to China on a book tour, for example, I researched communication and storytelling in modern and ancient Chinese culture. I identified three great communicators in Chinese history and analyzed their speeches. When I shared my analysis with audiences, it was clear to them that I understood the historical context surrounding the speeches—I could even provide detailed answers to their questions about it. I got feedback multiple times on that trip that people could see I cared enough to really study and understand their perspective.

Section 2
Message

Are ideas born interesting or made interesting?

—**Chip and Dan Heath,**
  authors of *Switch: How to Change Things When Change Is Hard*

Define Your
Big Idea

Your big idea is that one key message you *must* communicate. It's what compels the audience to change course. (Screenwriters call this the "controlling idea.") It has two components:

- **Your point of view:** The big idea needs to express *your* perspective on a subject, not a generalization like "Q4 financials." Otherwise, why present? You may as well e-mail your stakeholders a spreadsheet and be done with it.

- **What's at stake:** You'll also want to convey why the audience should care about your perspective. This helps people recognize their need to participate rather than continue with the status quo.

Express your big idea in a complete sentence. It needs a subject (often some version of "you," to highlight the audience's role) and a verb (to convey action and elicit emotion).

When asked, "What's your presentation about?" most people answer with a phrase like "Software updates." That's not a big idea; it's a topic—no point of view, no stakes. Change it to "Your department needs to update its workflow management software," and you're getting closer. You've added your point of view, but the stakes still aren't clear. So try this instead: "Your department will struggle to meet key production deadlines until we update the workflow management software."

Another example: If you say your presentation is about "the Florida wetlands," that's also just a topic. Add your point of view and what's at stake. For instance: "We need to restrict commercial and residential development in Florida's wetlands, because we're destroying the fragile ecosystem there and killing off endangered species."

People will move away from pain and toward pleasure. Prod them (with words like "struggle" from the first example; "destroying" and "killing" from the second) so they feel uncomfortable staying in their current position. Lure them toward your idea with encouragement and rewards (the promise of meeting deadlines; protection of endangered species).

Generate Content to Support the Big Idea

Now that you've articulated your big idea, it's time to create your content, but don't fire up your presentation software quite yet. Software forces linear thinking—one slide after another—so it's not the best tool for early brainstorming.

Instead, change up your usual environment. Move to a new room, turn off your e-mail and cell phone, maybe play some music. Use tactile tools like paper, whiteboards, and sticky notes.

Generate as many ideas as possible by:

- **Gathering existing content:** You don't have to start from scratch. Dig up other presentations, industry studies, news articles, reports, surveys—anything that's relevant to your big idea.

- **Building on existing content:** Push on the ideas in the content you've gathered. Challenge them, or consider them from a new angle. Draw new connections.

- **Creating new content:** Be curious, take risks, and let your intuition guide you. Experiment and dream.

For brainstorming to be successful, you have to suspend judgment and stay receptive to seemingly unrelated ideas—they may lead to something great. Increase your creative yield by moving back and forth between brainstorming alone and brainstorming in a group.

Brainstorm alone

It's intimidating to approach a blank piece of paper or whiteboard, but you have to start somewhere. Write down a key word and riff off that. Let your mind move in random directions. Then draw connections with lines. Keep brainstorming until you have a messy web of concepts and relationships to explore. This is called *mind mapping* (see figure 2-1). You can get special software to do it, but paper or sticky notes will work just as well.

Brainstorm in a group

When you work with others, you get more gems to choose from—and someone else's idea may spark even more creative ones in you. Be extra kind to the folks with enough guts to put half-baked or embarrassing ideas out there. Treat every idea as valuable. Have someone facilitate and capture the ideas so the discussion can move at a fast clip (if it slows down, people will start to question and censor themselves). Or ask brainstormers to scribble ideas on

FIGURE 2-1

Mind map

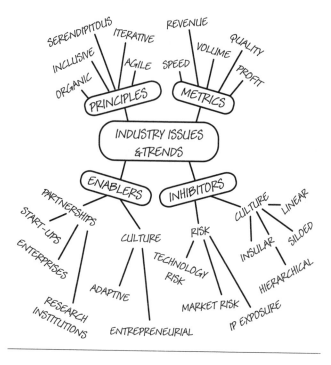

sticky notes and post them on a wall. Sticky notes are the perfect brainstorming tool. They're small, convenient, and moveable—great for collecting and organizing material. Limit yourselves to one idea per sticky note so it's easier to sort and cluster thoughts.

Brainstorm alone again

Take the seeds of ideas that came from the rapid-fire group session and do another round of quiet brainstorming on your own. This will give those latent ideas a chance to develop.

Go for quantity, not quality. You may work your way through five, ten, twenty ideas until you find ones that are distinctive and memorable. This is not the time to edit yourself. Even if an idea has been expressed or used before, add it to the mix. You may later find a unique way of incorporating it.

Anticipate Resistance

As a presenter, you're asking people to change their beliefs or behavior. That's not something they'll enjoy or find easy, so every audience will resist in some way. People will adamantly defend their own perspectives to avoid adopting yours. While listening to you, they'll catalog what they hear. Having come into the room with their own knowledge and biases, they'll constantly evaluate whether what you say fits within or falls outside their views.

So think through why and how they might resist, and plan accordingly. Here are the most common types of resistance, and how to get ready for them:

Logical resistance: Can you find logical arguments against your perspective? Dig up articles, blog posts, and reports that challenge your stance to familiarize yourself with alternate lines of reasoning. This kind of research prepares you for skeptical questions and comments you may have to field—and it helps you develop a deeper understanding of the topic and a more nuanced point of view.

Emotional resistance: Do the people you're addressing hold fast to a bias, dogma, or moral code—and does your idea violate that in some way? Hitting raw nerves will set off an audience, so proceed carefully. For example, if you're at a medical conference launching a new HPV vaccination for kids, also emphasize the importance of abstinence in youth.

Practical resistance: Is it physically or geographically difficult for the audience to do what you're asking? Will it take more financial means than people have? Be sensitive if you're asking employees to hang in there as you temporarily freeze salaries to weather a recession, for instance, or giving your team a deadline that will take nights and weekends to meet. Acknowledge the sacrifices people are making—and show that you're shouldering some of the burden yourself. Say that your salary will be frozen, too. Or explain that you'll be in 24/7 mode right along with your team until the big project is wrapped up—and that everyone will get comp time afterward.

Prepare for these types of resistance, and you'll stand a much better chance of winning over an entrenched audience. You can raise and address concerns before they become mental roadblocks—for example, by sharing at the beginning of your talk that you too were skeptical until you'd looked more closely at the data, or by meeting with particularly tough critics in advance to "pre-sell" your ideas. By showing that you've considered opposing points of view, you demonstrate an open mind—and invite your audience to respond in kind.

If you're struggling to come up with opposing viewpoints, share your big idea with others and ask them to pressure-test it. You may be so deeply connected to your perspective that you're having a hard time anticipating the most simple and obvious forms of resistance. Use your boss as a sounding board as you prepare to speak to the executive committee, for example. Or ask a key stakeholder for a reality check before you present to other managers in her group.

Amplify Your Message Through Contrast

People are naturally drawn to contrast because life is filled with it: Day and night. Male and female. Love and hate.

A skilled communicator captures an audience's interest by creating tension between contrasting elements—and then provides relief by resolving that tension. It's how you build a bridge between others' views and yours.

Try brainstorming ideas around polar opposites such as the ones in table 2-1.

TABLE 2-1

Dynamic opposites

Past/present	Future
Need	Fulfillment
Speed	Endurance
Ambition	Humility
Stagnation	Growth
Roadblocks	Clear passage
Sacrifice	Reward
Budget	Quality

Suppose you manage an airline's maintenance division, and you're asking for money to invest in analytics. Table 2-2 shows pairs of opposites you might explore as you figure out how to make your case.

TABLE 2-2

Using the tension of extremes

Customer complaints	Customer satisfaction
We're getting low ratings on customer surveys because of flight delays and missed connections caused by simple maintenance issues.	What if we could better schedule our planes' maintenance by digging into our repair data?
We currently follow the manufacturer's recommended maintenance schedule—and it's not sufficient. Planes get held up at the gate while mechanics do routine repairs.	By tracking and studying how often we actually perform certain kinds of repairs, we can create a schedule that's more realistic. We'll be able to prevent problems instead of fixing them when they pop up.

By embracing the tension between the extremes, you can propel your message—and the movement will feel natural.

The familiar will comfort people; the new will stimulate them and keep them interested. Generate plenty of content on both sides of the contrast or you'll lose momentum—and your audience.

Build an Effective Call to Action

Presentations move people to act—but only if you explicitly state what actions you want them to take, and when. Are you asking them to be doers, suppliers, influencers, or innovators (see table 2-3)?

To get to this list of four things an audience can do for you, I read hundreds of speeches and classified their calls to action. Whether your audience is corporate, political, scientific, or academic, the people you're addressing should fall into one of these categories.

Make it clear what you need to accomplish together and break that down into discrete tasks and deadlines that feel manageable to the audience. Let's consider an example where the call to action is to "innovate"—since that can be tough to pull off. Suppose you have an aging product that needs reinvention. Not all great ideas have to come from engineering. So after you say that the organization is open to ideas from all departments, you might break down the tasks like this:

- Identify enthusiastic brainstormers from all departments.

- Have engineers facilitate a cross-departmental brainstorming session that week.

- Assign a team member to take notes.

- Filter ideas at the engineering summit the following week.

You might ask everyone to take just one action, or you might provide a few actions people can choose from. Either way, be explicit in your request—and about how it will benefit the audience.

TABLE 2-3

What your audience can do for you

	Doers	Suppliers	Influencers	Innovators
What they do for you	Instigate activities	Get resources	Change perceptions	Generate ideas
How they do it	Doers are the worker bees. Once they know what needs to get done, they'll take on the tasks. They also recruit and motivate others to complete important activities.	Suppliers are the people with resources—financial, human, or material. They have the means to get you what you need to move forward.	Influencers can sway individuals or groups, large or small, mobilizing them to adopt and evangelize your idea.	Innovators think outside the box for new ways to add value to and spread your idea. They create strategies, perspectives, and products.

Choose Your Best Ideas

Up to this point, we've been focusing on how to generate presentation ideas and content. That's actually the easy part. It's much harder to trim everything down so only the most effective messages remain. But the quality of your presentation depends as much on what you choose to remove as on what you choose to include.

Many of your ideas may be fascinating and clever, but you can't fit them all in—and no one wants to hear them all, anyway. Connect, analyze, sort, and filter the ideas so you use only the ones that will yield the best outcomes. Designers call this part of the process *convergent thinking*, and they refer to its opposite, idea generation, as *divergent thinking* (see figure 2-2). As Tim Brown, the CEO of IDEO, explains: "In the divergent phase, new options emerge. In the convergent phase, it is just the reverse. Now it's time to eliminate options and make choices."

Your primary filter should be your big idea (see "Define Your Big Idea" at the beginning of the Message section). Everything you keep in your talk must support it.

FIGURE 2-2

Filter your best ideas

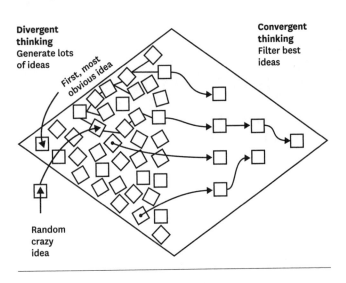

If you don't filter your presentation, the audience will have to—and people will resent you for making them work too hard to identify the most important points. Cut mercilessly on their behalf. Say you're presenting a business case for acquiring a company. You might brainstorm things to cover, like:

- The competencies your company would gain

- Estimated return on investment

- Lessons learned from the last acquisition

- Threat R&D might perceive

- Bringing in culture consultants

- Receivables are at net 45 days

- Need to retool the factory floor

All these ideas fit into the big idea except the fact that receivables are at net 45 days. Though that may be important, it would be a distraction during this meeting. Save it for another meeting.

Even if all you do is sort and filter the ideas you've generated, you're technically ready to present. You can place your sticky notes on the inside of a file folder and use those as your speaking notes, as I did at a launch party for my book *Resonate*. I had only to glance down once in a while.

Or you can begin to put your ideas into the presentation software of your choice.

Organize Your Thoughts

Because presentation programs such as PowerPoint are visual tools, we often jump too quickly into visually expressing our ideas when we use them—before we've spent enough time arranging our thoughts and crafting our words. When moving ideas from sticky notes to software, enter each point you plan to cover as a clearly worded title in outline or slide-sorter mode rather than going straight to slide-creation mode (figure 2-3). That allows you to read the titles in sequence, without the distractions of supporting details or graphics, to make sure your presentation flows from point to point.

Ask yourself, "If people read just the titles, will they get what I'm saying?" That's not just an academic exercise. You really want to know the answer, because your audience members often won't read past your slide titles when you present. They'll scan them the way they do headlines of news articles—and make snap decisions

FIGURE 2-3

Convey a clear message with each title

about whether they'd like to learn more. So convey a clear message with each title, arrange them in an order that will make sense to your audience, and infuse them with personality where you can. You'll want to come across as a real person, not an automaton. Include verbs to show action.

Compare the examples shown in table 2-4.

TABLE 2-4

Convey clear meaning with titles

Vague, passive	Clear, active
Market overview	We're neck-and-neck with an aggressive rival.
Productivity gains	Production time shrank from 21 days to 8.

Agonize over your titles as marketing copywriters do in their campaigns to get more click-throughs and sales. You, too, are selling something—your big idea—and the more quickly you grab people's attention, the higher your "conversion rate" will be.

Balance Analytical and Emotional Appeal

Now that you've outlined your message, consider how you'll appeal to people's minds and hearts.

Strike the wrong balance of analytical and emotional content in your presentation, and you risk alienating the audience and diminishing your credibility. But how do you get it right? Take your cues from the topic and the audience.

Certain topics—like layoffs and product launches—are inherently charged and naturally lend themselves to emotional appeal. Others—like science, engineering, and finance—invite more analytic treatment.

Weigh the subject against the group you're addressing. Suppose you're making a case for personnel cuts to a group of managers who'll soon have to decide which direct reports to let go. They may see you as cold and inhumane if you focus primarily on cost savings, with nary a word about people losing jobs. A numbers-based approach will probably go over better with a group of executives charged with improving the bottom line—though even they will expect you to at least acknowledge that layoffs are difficult.

No presentation should be devoid of emotional content, no matter how cerebral the topic or the audience. In a business setting, it may feel more comfortable to just "state the facts," but look through your deck and see if you can add emotional texture to any content that's purely analytical (see figure 2-4).

FIGURE 2-4

Strike a balance

Analytical	Emotional
Features	Benefits illustrated through stories (personal, true, fictional)
Data/evidence	
Exhibits	Metaphors and analogies that make data meaningful
Logical arguments	
Proofs	Thought-provoking questions
Examples	
Case studies	Slow reveal (builds suspense)

There are two basic classes of emotion: pain and pleasure. Determine how you'd like people to feel at various points in your presentation. Where would you like them to feel happy? To cringe? To be inspired?

Ask "why" questions to unearth your big idea's emotional appeal. For example, if you're requesting funding to pay for cloud storage, start by asking, "Why do we need to buy cloud storage?" Your answer may be "to facilitate data sharing with colleagues in remote locations." So then ask, "Why do we need to facilitate data sharing with colleagues in remote locations?" Eventually you'll get to the human beings whose lives will be affected by your idea, and that's where you'll discover your emotional appeal: Maybe you need cloud storage "to help those remote colleagues coordinate disaster relief efforts and save lives."

Once you know what that hook is, use words or phrases that have emotional weight to them—like "save lives" in the cloud example above. Tell personal stories with conviction and describe not just what people did, but how they felt. (See "Add Emotional Texture" in the Story section of this guide.)

Lose the Jargon

Have you ever listened to a presenter who sounded supersmart—without having any idea what she *really* said?

Each field has its own lexicon, filled with words that are familiar to experts but foreign to everyone else. Even different departments within the same organization use niche language and acronyms that mean nothing to other groups. And the more companies and individuals innovate within their areas of expertise, the bigger and gnarlier their vocabularies get.

Unless you're presenting to a roomful of specialists cut from the same cloth, don't assume that everyone will understand your jargon. Modify your language so it resonates with the people whose support and influence you need. If they can't follow your ideas, they won't adopt them.

What's more, delivering abstruse presentations can hurt your career. As communications coach Carmine Gallo puts it, "Speaking over people's heads may cost you a job or prevent you from advancing as far as your capabilities might take you otherwise."

So lose the jargon. If a specialized term is central to your message, translate it. Would your grandmother understand what you're talking about? Rework your message until it's *that clear.*

The presenter in the following example (figure 2-5) spoke to an audience of 800 people who could fund his

FIGURE 2-5

Drop the jargon

Before: Developed from a scientific perspective	After: Reworked for a lay audience
I am currently the lead researcher developing a microbially induced brine-mining technology, where bacteria are employed to accumulate selected minerals from desalination brine, producing a minable sediment, which may indirectly reduce the cost of desalinated water and the environmental impact of the desalination process.	Desalination is a process that removes salt from water so it can be used for drinking and irrigation. Removing salt from water—in particular sea water—via reverse osmosis requires energy to produce clean water. This process also creates a toxic saltwater solution, or brine, that is generally dumped back out at sea and is harmful for the ecology of the receiving water body.
Initial experiments have shown how certain bacterial cultures are able to mine selected metals from desalination brine. I am now hoping to prove the economic viability of the process through qualitative and quantitative studies of the metals produced.	This is where my collaboration with bacteria comes in. Introducing bacteria into the brine draws out metals such as calcium, potassium, and magnesium from desalination brine. The value of magnesium alone in the volume of brine potentially needed for Singapore represents 4.5 billon U.S. dollars—indirectly lowering the cost of the desalinated water produced, while reducing the environmental impact of the process.
Conventional mechanical and chemical mining technologies are restrictive due to technological and economic constraints. Biological processes, however, present an efficient and environmentally benign alternative, which must be seen in the context of a future where urban ecological systems are in harmony with the ecological cycles of our planet.	Imagine a mining industry in a way it hasn't existed before.
	Imagine a mining industry that doesn't mean defiling the earth.
	Imagine bacteria helping us achieve this industry, as they accumulate and sediment minerals out of desalination brine.
	In other words, imagine a mining industry in harmony with nature.

idea but didn't have deep knowledge of the science behind it. The first column shows what he said during rehearsal; the second shows what he said at the presentation, after he got feedback and reworked his talk for an intelligent lay audience.

Craft Sound Bites

Your words are now clear—but are they memorable? Will people share them with others?

Great quotes get picked up and repeated—whether at the water cooler, in blog posts, or on social networking sites. Brilliant ones end up on the front pages of newspapers. So embed well-crafted sound bites into every talk.

Steve Jobs made this an art form. He relied on rhetorical devices to drive his messages home and get pickup from audiences and press alike. Here are a few that he used to great effect:

Rhythmic repetition: **Repeated phrase at beginning, middle, or end of a sentence.**

In 2010, Jobs had to deliver an emergency press conference about the performance of the antenna in the iPhone 4. If users held the phone a certain way, it dropped calls. As social media scientist Dan Zarrella, at HubSpot, points out, Jobs repeated the phrase "We want to make all our users happy" several times during his talk. Midway through, Jobs flashed a slide showing that the antenna issue affected only a fraction of users. Soon, a message appeared at the bottom: "We care about *every* user." A few slides later: "We love our users." Then "We love our users" appeared again on the next slide. And the next. And the next. "We love our users, we love them," Jobs concluded. "We do this [provide a free phone case that will solve the problem] because we love our users." That "love" was the message the press took away from his piece of "crisis communication."

Concrete comparison: Simile or metaphor.

In his iPhone keynote speech at MacWorld 2007, Jobs likened Apple's switch to Intel processors to a "huge *heart transplant.*"

Slogan: A concise statement that's easy to remember.

At the iPhone launch, Jobs said "reinvent the phone" several times—and the slogan was all over the press release Apple sent out before his keynote. "Reinvent the phone" ended up in *PCWorld*'s headlines the next day.

As Jobs did, take time to create repeatable sound bites. But don't deliver them with a lot of fanfare. Make them appear spontaneous, so people will *want* to repeat them.

Section 3
Story

[Stories] are the currency of human contact.

—**Robert McKee,**
 author of *Story: Substance, Structure, Style, and the
 Principles of Screenwriting*

Apply Storytelling Principles

Stories have the power to win customers, align colleagues, and motivate employees. They're the most compelling platform we have for managing imaginations. Those who master this art form can gain great influence and an enduring legacy.

If you use stories in your presentation, the audience can recall what they've learned from you and even spread the word. Just as the plot of a compelling play, movie, or novel makes a writer's themes more vivid and memorable, well-crafted stories can give your message real staying power, for two key reasons:

- **Stories feature transformation:** When people hear a story, they root for the protagonist as she overcomes obstacles and emerges changed in some important way (perhaps a new outlook helps her complete a difficult physical journey). It's doubly powerful to incorporate stories that demonstrate how others have adopted the same beliefs and behaviors you're proposing—that is, show others going through a similar transformation that your audience will go through. This will help you get people to cross over from their everyday world into the world of your ideas—and come back to their world transformed, with new insights and tools from your presentation.

- **Stories have a clear structure:** All effective stories adhere to the same basic three-part structure that Aristotle pointed out ages ago: They have a beginning, a middle, and an end. It makes them easy to digest and retell—and it's how audiences have been conditioned for centuries to receive information. Make sure your presentation—and any story you tell within it—has all three parts, with clear transitions between them.

In this section of the guide, you'll learn how to use storytelling principles to structure your presentation and incorporate anecdotes that add emotional appeal.

Create a Solid Structure

All good presentations—like all good stories—convey and resolve some kind of conflict or imbalance. The sense of discord is what makes audiences care enough to get on board.

After gleaning story insights from films and books, studying hundreds of speeches, and spending 22 years creating customized presentations for companies and thought leaders, I've found that the most persuasive communicators create conflict by juxtaposing *what is* with *what could be.* That is, they alternately build tension and provide release by toggling back and forth between the status quo and a better way—finally arriving at the "new bliss" people will discover by adopting the proposed beliefs and behaviors. That conflict resolution plays out within the basic beginning-middle-end storytelling structure we all know and love (figure 3-1).

The tips in this section will help you weave conflict and resolution throughout the beginning, middle, and end of your presentation.

FIGURE 3-1

Persuasive story pattern

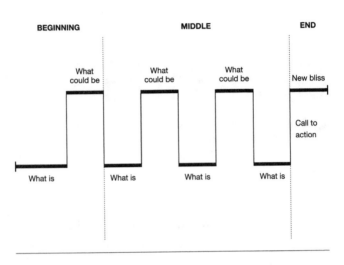

Craft the Beginning

Begin by describing life as the audience knows it. People should be nodding their heads in recognition because you're articulating what they already understand. This creates a bond between you and them and opens them up to hear your ideas for change.

After you set that baseline of *what is*, introduce your ideas of *what could be*. The gap between the two will throw the audience a bit off balance, and that's a good thing—because it creates tension that needs to be resolved (figure 3-2).

FIGURE 3-2

Create dramatic tension

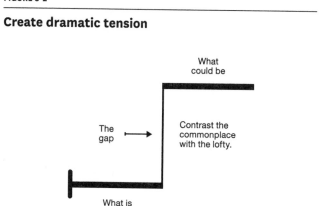

67

If you proposed what could be without first establishing what is, you'd fail to connect with the audience before swooping in with your ideas, and your message would lose momentum.

The gap shouldn't feel contrived—you wouldn't say "Okay, I've described what is. Now let's move to what could be." Present it naturally so people will feel moved, not manipulated. For instance:

What is: We're fell short of our Q3 financial goals partly because we're understaffed and everyone's spread too thin.

What could be: But what if we could solve the worst of our problems by bringing in a couple of powerhouse clients? Well, we can.

Here's another example:

What is: Analysts have been placing our products at the top of three out of five categories. One competitor just shook up the industry with the launch of its T3xR—heralded as the most innovative product in our space. Analysts predict that firms like ours will have no future unless we license this technology from our rival.

What could be: But we will not concede! In fact, we will retain our lead. I'm pleased to tell you that five years ago we had the same product idea, but after rapid prototyping we discovered a way to leapfrog that generation of technology. So today, we're launching a product so revolutionary that we'll gain a ten-year lead in our industry.

Once you establish the gap between what is and what could be, use the remainder of the presentation to bridge it.

Develop the Middle

The middle is, in many ways, the most compelling part of your presentation, because that's where most of the "action" takes place.

People in your audience now realize their world is off-kilter—you've brought that to their attention and at least hinted at a solution at the beginning of your presentation. Now continue to emphasize the contrast between what is and what could be, moving back and forth between them, and the audience will start to find the former unappealing and the latter alluring.

Let's go back to that Q3 financial update example from "Craft the Beginning." Revenues are down, but you want to motivate employees to make up for it. Table 3-1 shows one way you could approach the middle of your presentation.

Earlier, you brainstormed around pairs of contrasting themes (see "Amplify Your Message Through Contrast" in the Message section). Try using one of those pairs—for instance, sacrifice versus reward—to drum up material to flesh out this structure.

Creating "action" in the middle of your story

What is	What could be
We missed our Q3 forecast by 15%.	Q4 numbers must be strong for us to pay out bonuses.
We have six new clients on our roster.	Two of them have the potential to bring in more revenue than our best clients do now.
The new clients will require extensive retooling in manufacturing.	We'll be bringing in experts from Germany to help.

Make the Ending Powerful

Your ending should leave people with a heightened sense of what could be—and willingness to believe or do something new. Here's where you describe how blissful their world will be when they adopt your ideas.

Let's return to our Q3 example from "Craft the Beginning" and "Develop the Middle" in this section. You might wrap up your presentation along the lines of figure 3-3.

FIGURE 3-3

Making the ending powerful

Call to action	New bliss
It will take extra work from all departments to make Q4 numbers, but we can deliver products to our important new clients on time and with no errors.	I know everyone's running on fumes—but hang in there. This is our chance to pull together like a championship team, and things will get easier if we make this work. The reward if we meet our Q4 targets? Bonuses, plus days off at the end of the year.

Many presentations simply end with a list of action items, but that isn't exactly inspiring. You want the last thing you say to move your audience to tackle those items. You want people to feel ready to right the wrong, to conquer the problem.

By skillfully defining future rewards, you compel people to get on board with your ideas. Show them that taking action will be worth their effort. Highlight:

- **Benefits to them:** What needs of theirs will your ideas meet? What freedoms will the audience gain? How will your ideas give the audience greater influence or status?

- **Benefits to their "sphere":** How will your ideas help the audience's peers, direct reports, customers, students, or friends?

- **Benefits to the world:** How will your ideas help the masses? How will they improve public health, for instance, or help the environment?

In the example above, we've called out a key benefit to the organization (making up for Q3 revenue shortfall), plus three benefits to employees (bonuses, time off, and—probably most important—the promise of a saner workload).

Add Emotional Texture

Now step back and review all your content so far. Do you have the right mix of analysis and emotion? (See "Balance Analytical and Emotional Appeal" in the Message section.) If you need more emotional impact, you can add it with storytelling.

A message matters to people when it hits them in the gut. Visceral response, not pure analysis, is what will push your audience away from the status quo and toward your perspective. Stories elicit that kind of response. When we hear stories, our eyes dilate, our hearts race, we feel chills. We laugh, clap, lean forward or back. These reactions are mostly involuntary, because they're grounded in emotion.

While you're describing what is, tell a story that makes people shudder, or guffaw at the ridiculousness of their situation, or feel disappointment. While you're describing what could be, tell a story that strikes a little awe or fear into their hearts—something that inspires them to change.

Table 3-2 shows a template (with an example plugged in) that can help you transform supporting information into a story with emotional impact.

You may be thinking that people don't go to work to feel; they go to get stuff done. But by making them feel, you move them to action—and help them get stuff done. It's not about issuing a gushing, weepy plea. It's about

TABLE 3-2

Making an emotional impact with data

Point you want to make	Every cross-divisional function could benefit from a steering committee.	
STORY ABOUT ORGANIZATIONAL CHANGE		
Beginning	When, who, where	A few years ago, the sales team tackled a cross-divisional problem with the help of a steering committee.
Middle	Context	At the time, all sales groups were independent.
	Conflict	This means we were confusing customers with many different rules, processes, and formats.
	Proposed resolution	So we decided to create a sales steering committee.
	Complication	You can imagine how hard it was to reach agreement on anything.
End	Actual resolution	But we agreed to meet every two weeks to find common ground. Over the next year, we standardized all our processes and learned a lot from each other. The customers became much happier with our service.

Source: Glenn Hughes, SMART as Hell.

adding emotional texture to the logical case you've built with data, case studies, and other supporting evidence.

Personal stories told with conviction are the most effective ones in your arsenal. You can repeat stories you've heard, but audiences feel more affection for presenters who reveal their own challenges and vulnerability.

Use relevant stories that are appropriately dramatic, or you may come across as manipulative or out of touch with reality. When giving an update at a small staff meeting on a project you're leading, you wouldn't tell a melodramatic story about the "just-in-time delivery" of multiple vendors you managed at your daughter's wedding. It would waste everyone's time.

But one U.S. government official *did* effectively tell a story about his daughter's wedding—to get new remote-communication technology adopted in his organization. Many of his relatives couldn't travel to the wedding, so he used a commercial version of the technology to push the wedding pictures quickly to the remote family members, helping all feel more included in the event. He argued that adopting the enterprise version of this technology would similarly include distant employees in the development of important agency initiatives. The senior executives not only understood this with their minds but felt it in their hearts. They could relate this story about a father doing his best to serve his family to their agency doing its best to serve the citizenry.

Take out a notepad and start cataloging personal stories and the emotions they summon. This exercise takes time, but it will yield material you can draw on again and again. Do your first pass when you have an uninterrupted hour or so to reflect. You can use the checklist that follows to trigger your memory. As you recall past events, jot down how you felt when you experienced them.

Inventory of Personal Stories

- ☐ *Important times in your life:* Childhood, adolescence, young adulthood, later years

- ☐ *Relatives:* Parents, grandparents, siblings, children, in-laws

- ☐ *Authority figures:* Teachers, bosses, coaches, mentors, leaders, political figures, other influencers

- ☐ *Peers:* Colleagues, social networks, club members, friends, neighbors, teammates

- ☐ *Subordinates:* Employees, mentees, trainees, interns, volunteers, students

- ☐ *Enemies:* Competitors, bullies, people with challenging personalities, people you've been hurt by, people you've hurt

- ☐ *Important places:* Offices, homes, schools, places of worship, local hangouts, camps, vacation spots, foreign lands

- ☐ *Things you cherish:* Gifts, photos, certificates/awards, keepsakes

- ☐ *Things that have injured you:* Sharp objects, animal bites, spoiled food, allergens

Spending time with each item on this list, you'll unearth many stories you've forgotten. Even after you've selected stories for whatever presentation you're currently working on, save your notes and continue adding to them here and there, as you find time. They'll come in handy when you're creating future presentations.

Use Metaphors as Your Glue

Metaphors are a powerful literary device. In Dr. Martin Luther King Jr.'s "I Have a Dream" speech, about 20% of what he said was metaphorical. For example, he likened his lack of freedom to a bad check that "America has given the Negro people . . . a check which has come back marked 'insufficient funds.'" King introduced this metaphor three minutes into his 16-minute talk, and it was the first time the audience roared and clapped.

Presenters tend to overrely on tired visual metaphors instead of using powerful words to stir hearts. King's speech would not have been nearly as beautiful if he'd used slides with pictures of bad checks and piles of gold symbolizing "freedom and the security of justice."

For each point you make in your presentation, try to come up with a metaphor to connect people's minds to the concept. You might even weave it like a thread throughout the presentation.

When developing metaphors, reject overused themes like racecars and sporting events—and avoid stock photos along those lines. If you want to tell a story of triumph, dig into one of your own stories for the right metaphor: Describe, for instance, how it felt to struggle to the top of Yosemite's Half Dome, run your first marathon, or win the citywide Boy Scout trophy. Identify metaphors that will be meaningful to the audience.

Create Something They'll Always Remember

Place *Something They'll Always Remember*—a climactic S.T.A.R. moment—in your presentation to drive your big idea home. That moment is what the audience will chat (or tweet) about after your talk. It can also help your message go viral through social media and news coverage. Use it to make people uncomfortable with what is or to draw them toward what could be. Here are four ways to create a S.T.A.R. moment that captivates your audience and generates buzz.

Shocking statistics

If statistics are shocking, don't glide over them—amplify them. For example, in his 2010 Consumer Electronics Show presentation, Intel CEO Paul Otellini used startling numbers to convey the speed and impact of the company's newest technology. "Today we have the industry's first-shipping 32-nanometer process technology. A

32-nanometer microprocessor is 5,000 times faster; its transistors are 100,000 times cheaper than the 4004 processor that we began with. With all respect to our friends in the auto industry, if their products had produced the same kind of innovation, cars today would go 470,000 miles per hour. They'd get 100,000 miles per gallon, and they'd cost three cents."

Evocative visuals

Audiences connect with emotionally potent visuals. When asking donors to help raise $1.7 million, Conservation International contrasted dreamy, glistening, surreal under-ocean images (captioned with phrases like "90% of our oxygen" describing how dependent we are on the ocean) with photos of grimy rubbish that washes up on the beach (where "14 billion pounds of trash" roll in on the waves). That approach tapped the power of evocative visuals and shocking stats—and people responded by getting out their wallets.

Memorable dramatization

Bring your message to life by dramatizing it. As Bill Gates spoke about the importance of malaria eradication at a TED conference in 2009, he released a jar of mosquitoes into the auditorium and said, "There is no reason only poor people should be infected." It got the audience's attention—and effectively made the point that we don't spend nearly enough money on fighting the disease. The mosquitoes were malaria-free, but he let people squirm a minute or two before he let them know that.

Consider another example. When Mirran Raphaely, CEO of Dr. Hauschka Skin Care, presented to the cosmetics industry, she wanted to draw a sharp contrast between industrial agriculture and biodynamic farming practices. She showed two photos side by side—a container of chemicals and an herb called horsetail—and compared the toxicity of the two substances. In industrial agriculture, farmers rely on glyphosate, a synthetic chemical linked to cancer in animals and humans. In biodynamic agriculture, farmers treat crops with an extract made from horsetail. Holding up two glasses—one filled with the chemical weed killer, the other with the horsetail extract—she asked the audience, "Which one of these would you want on the crops you consume?" After the audience finished laughing, she took a sip of the biodynamic solution.

Emotive anecdote

Sometimes S.T.A.R. moments are gripping personal stories (see "Add Emotional Texture" earlier in this section).

Here's one such story, told by Symantec.cloud group president Rowan Trollope in May 2012, to encourage his organization to innovate:

> I went mountain climbing at Mount Laurel, in the eastern Sierras, with two of my friends. I'm not very experienced, but both of them were even less experienced. We'd been climbing for about 19 hours. We were up at 11,000 feet, and it was getting dark. Fast.
>
> We needed to get down the side of this mountain . . . and we needed to do it fast. Descending first, I got to a ledge and started to get our line ready.
>
> Climbers carry two emergency pitons with them for just this purpose. I'd never used them before, but I knew

how they worked. I took out my hammer and started hammering one into the rock. The books tell you that you'll hear the tone of the hammer strike change when it's "in." I heard a loud ping with each strike of the hammer and decided it was in "good enough."

The books also tell you, though, to always use two, so I used two. As I hammered in the second one, I heard a sharp, high-pitched ping at the end, so I tied the knots and got our line ready. By this time, my buddies had reached the ledge, and I started to hook us in.

Something was bugging me. I looked at the knot between the two pitons and it looked like this [prop: climbing rope with two pitons]. The problem with a knot like that is that if one piton fails, you'll fall. You need to tie it instead like this [prop: retie knot].

My buddies were all clipped in and wanted to get going. It was getting darker. The way I tied the knot seemed good enough, but something in the back of my head told me to stop. So I did.

We all unclipped, and I retied the knot, and then we clipped in again and started the climb down.

The moment I put weight on my line, the first piton popped out and hit me smack in the middle of the helmet. Had I not unclipped and retied the knot, I would have died on that ledge. My life rushed through my mind. And I suddenly and irrevocably got the danger of "good enough."

When I pounded in that first piton, I decided it was good enough.

When I tied the knot that first time, I decided that it wasn't, so I did it again.

I still have that piton that popped out. I brought it with me today because I thought you might like to see it [prop: piton]. The other one? The one that saved my life? It's still in a crack on the Laurel Cliffs. Still doing its job.

I came back to work, and everything had new meaning for me. Retying my knots became a sort of metaphor. I realized that in every job I did, every project I touched, I was making piton decisions every time. I was deciding, with every one of those moves, whether good enough was good enough for me.

I picked that story for today because I think we're facing a similar climb as a company. And we're making piton decisions every day. For my buddies and me, there was nothing but sky beneath us. When you and I look down, we see the PC business changing dramatically. We can see physical things being driven into the cloud, and we can agree that the Internet is not yet a secure place.

Unfortunately, it will take more than one piton to address these dangers. But I think it starts by reawakening in our company some of the qualities that made us great in the first place. And to do that, I think we need to change how we approach our work.

Section 4
Media

People who know what they're talking about don't need PowerPoint.

—Steve Jobs

Choose the Right Vehicle for Your Message

Now that you've carefully considered your audience's needs and tailored your message and content accordingly, it's time to determine how the people you're addressing prefer to process information so you can select the best vehicle for reaching them. Just because you have something to communicate and a time slot to fill doesn't mean a formal presentation with slides is the right choice. Some audiences—a group of analysts, for example—may find a thoughtfully written memo more persuasive. Others, such as young professionals, might prefer a video.

It's your job to determine the best way to connect with your audience. Presentations aren't limited to a single time or place anymore. They can be broadcasted, streamed, downloaded, and distributed. Slides aren't a must-have, either. You can use props, handouts, sketches, tablets, videos, flipcharts—pretty much anything that will help people receive your message.

Before opening your presentation software, think about your audience and venue. Will you be speaking to a few team members in an intimate setting? A big crowd in an auditorium? A small group who will be connecting remotely? The size of your audience and the level of interaction that your setting allows should determine which media you choose.

See figure 4-1 for a sampling of ideas on how to deliver your message to one person or many, in a staged or more spontaneous setting.

There's also an element of common sense. Delivering a stand-up formal presentation in a small conference room just doesn't make sense if you're speaking to two of your direct reports—but it does if you're speaking to a couple of venture capitalists who may invest in your business.

Although technology has opened up new ways of communicating, a low-tech approach is sometimes your best bet. If you show up with a slick slide deck, everything seems final. But sketching out ideas while people watch and listen signals that your thinking is in the formative stages and that the audience can still weigh in.

Maybe the "presentation" you're developing should really be a carefully mapped-out conversation with a planned whiteboard drawing. When my firm was buying a new digital storage system, we met with two potential vendors: One brought a deck of slides and didn't deviate from its spiel. The other, which won our business, whiteboarded out a full storage and network plan. That rep came across as having listened to our needs and understood what we wanted. Her presentation felt collaborative, not canned.

FIGURE 4-1

Choosing your delivery style

Casual   staged   Formal

(1:1) Small audience (1:few)

(1:many) Large audience (few:many)

Interactive   spontaneous   Canned

Carefully planned but informally delivered

- Deliver short presentation, then discuss
- Lead conversation with planned whiteboard sketches
- Lead conference call with document or slides posted (earnings call)

Programmed, staged, and formally rehearsed

- Deliver formal presentation with polished visuals
- Host panel discussion
- Host formal webinar (audience is muted)

Facilitated by presenter or audience

- Distribute printed document or slides, then meet to discuss
- Host conversational webinar (audience is unmuted)
- Use flipchart or whiteboard spontaneously

Distributed for audience to access on own time

- Package or stream on-demand presentation
- Post slides with audio voice-over or recorded webinar
- Post curated content (slides, videos, articles, white papers)

Make the Most of Slide Software

Presentation software is widely reviled. The press has called PowerPoint evil, and corporations have cried for its banishment. The software isn't at fault. It's an empty shell, a container for our ideas. It's not a bad communication tool unless it's in the hands of a bad communicator.

So how do you use it without abusing it—and your audience? Know exactly what you're trying to accomplish and rely on the software to achieve that—and nothing more.

You can use presentation software to create documents, compose teleprompter notes, and visualize ideas. But keep those tasks *separate* to avoid the most common PowerPoint pitfalls. The trick is to show audience members only what they want to see, when they want to see it.

Create documents

Presentation software is great for laying out dense material in easy-to-read documents. In fact, that functionality is built right in—the default setting is a document template, not a slide template. You can swiftly compose and format your text and move sections around—and best of all, when it's time to derive a presentation from that document, you don't have to copy and paste from Word.

That said, don't *project* your entire document when you speak. No one wants to attend a plodding read-along. It's boring, and people can read more efficiently on their own, anyway. Circulate your document before or after the presentation so you won't need to project text-heavy slides—which Garr Reynolds, author of *Presentation Zen*, aptly calls *slideuments*. If your content can be distributed and clearly understood without a presenter, you've created a document, not a presentation—and that's fine as long as you treat it as such. That might be all you need if you're giving a status update, for instance.

If you step back and realize you've created a slideument, it may be a sign that you need to distribute a document. Make some adjustments so it looks and feels more like a document before you circulate it. Try dividing the content into clear sections, creating a table of contents that links to each one, adding page numbers, converting fragments and phrases into complete sentences, and distributing the file as a PDF rather than a slide deck. Nolan Haims, the presentation director at the global PR firm Edelman, sets up slideuments in portrait layout instead of landscape so it's very clear to staff members that they're documents in the making, not visual aids to be projected.

Compose teleprompter notes

What if you have to deliver several presentations per month, each customized for a different audience? (Think of sales pitches tailored to corporate clients, for example.) In situations like that, it's impossible to memorize what you'll say every time—and you shouldn't have to.

For decades, great orators have relied on note cards, notepaper, even full scripts. You can use bulleted slides as teleprompter material—but again, *don't project them.* You'll run into the same read-along problems (boredom and inefficiency) you encounter when you project slide-uments. Sheryl Sandberg, the COO of Facebook, didn't show any slides at her eloquent TEDWomen presentation "Why We Have Too Few Women Leaders." But when the camera panned to her view of the audience, you could see her bulleted slides on the comfort monitor. Those slides were her teleprompter notes, and she was the only person in the room viewing them.

If you're using PowerPoint to compose teleprompter notes, write them in "Notes" view, and then go to "Set Up Show." After you attach your projector, select "Presenter View." Everything in your notes will appear on your laptop screen or comfort monitor, and only your slides will project behind you. Bring printouts of your teleprompter notes in case anything technical goes wrong.

Visualize ideas

The only things you should actually project are images, graphics, and phrases that move your ideas along—and cement them in the audience's memory long after your presentation is over. Strip everything off your slides that's there to remind you what to say; keep only elements that will help the audience understand and retain what you're saying. Developing clear visuals that add emotion, emphasis, or nuance to your delivery is no easy task—but when you do this well, your ideas will resonate with your audience. (See the Slides section in this guide for detailed tips on creating powerful visual aids.)

Determine the Right Length for Your Presentation

If you ask around, "What do great presentations have in common?" you'll get one consistent answer: "They're short." It's no secret that people value their time.

But many presenters don't realize that it costs *them* time to save the audience time. It's easier to blather on for an hour than to craft a tight, succinct presentation. Some of the magic of TED is in the 18-minute limit. A great talk goes by quickly. A bad one—well, people can endure it if it's only 18 minutes.

People in your audience won't scold you for ending early, but they will for ending late. Out of consideration for them and the day's agenda, treat the time slot assigned to you as sacred. And keep in mind that people have a 30- to 40-minute presentation tolerance (they're conditioned by TV shows with creatively produced commercial breaks). Go longer than that, and they'll begin to squirm.

Here are five ways to tighten your talk and keep your audience engaged:

1. **Plan content for 60% of your time slot:** If you're given a full hour, take no more than 40 minutes. That will leave time for Q&A, a panel, or some other form of discussion. It's hard to keep people's attention for much longer than 40 minutes unless you've built in interesting guest speakers, video clips, interactive exercises, and such. As Thomas Jefferson put it, "Speeches that are measured by the hour will die with the hour."

2. **Trim your slide deck:** If you created an hour-long presentation and want to deliver it in 40 minutes, cut your slides by a third. You can work in slide-sorter mode in PowerPoint, dragging slides to a "slide cemetery" at the very end of the file. Don't delete them, because you might have to resurrect one or more at the last minute, when you're answering questions.

3. **Practice with the clock counting up:** As you're cutting material, rehearse with a clock counting up, not with a timer counting down. If you go over, you need to know how much you're over. Give critical content the most stage time; cut sections that are more important to you than to the audience. Keep trimming and practicing until you're consistently within your desired time frame.

4. **Practice with a timer counting down:** Once you're within the time frame, begin practicing with a timer counting down. Divide your content into quarters and calculate a time stamp for the end of each quarter. For example, if you're giving a 40-minute talk, know the exact slide you should be on at the 10-, 20-, and 30-minute marks so you can gauge throughout the talk if you're on time or running over. That way you can trim more easily on the fly.

5. **Have two natural ending points:** Create a false ending (a summary of the ideas covered, for example) and a real ending—perhaps a rousing, inspirational story that drives the message home. If you're running long, you can drop the second ending and still get your message across. Once at a TED event in India, I was given a 15-minute time slot and had rehearsed it to a T. Two days before the talk, I caught a severe chest cold, so I was heavily medicated when I walked on stage. Before I knew it, the "time's up" light was blinking, and I wasn't done. Fortunately, I'd planned two natural places to end my talk, so I wrapped things up with my first ending, citing a beautiful salutation to the land of India from a famous Indian speech. As far as the people in the audience knew, that was the real ending—and they responded warmly.

Persuade Beyond the Stage

Your presentation doesn't start the moment you enter the room; it starts the moment you've committed to speak—and it continues after the actual talk, as you follow up with the audience. If you take advantage of opportunities to reinforce your message at all three stages, you're much more likely to change people's thinking and behavior.

Before

How you position the talk before you even deliver it will have a big impact on the audience's level of interest. Consider the most effective forms of communication to send out in advance. If you're presenting to colleagues, you might e-mail them a summary of your message and a rough list of points you plan to cover, for example, or send a meeting request with a detailed agenda. If you're going to speak to people from outside your organization—conference attendees, for instance—you may post your biography and talking points online and provide links to prereading material (published articles, abstracts of white papers, and so on).

Preparing strong supporting material may take as long as developing the presentation itself. However you choose to orient your audience members, make it clear how they will benefit from this talk.

During

If you need to distribute handouts during your talk, bring more than enough copies and recruit volunteers to pass them out at the right time. You can also tape secret messages under people's chairs for retrieval at a key moment during your talk, have audience members hold up color-coded cards to give you feedback in real time, or give them all a prop to interact with, such as a product prototype.

And if you're trying to create external buzz—about a launch, for example—post your slides online along with any videos or photos that support your presentation. Downloadable assets like these will make it easier for journalists, bloggers, and fans in social media circles to write about your talk. If appropriate, use webinar or streaming technology to further increase your audience reach.

After

Follow up with a thank-you note, a survey, or supplementary reading or viewing material to keep your message fresh in people's minds. But don't overtly solicit your audience. People should feel they're getting additional insights and value—not doing extra work that benefits you more than it does them. For example, if you send a survey to find out what they think about a new service you're offering, make it worth their time: Explain how their feedback will lead to benefits they'll care about, and offer a relevant, attractive free product in exchange for their participation. When I wrap up a webinar on presentations, I set up a URL where the audience can access free digital content from my books on the topic. Attendees love getting free, useful tools like this. More than a quarter of them download the files.

By adding points of contact before, during, and after your presentation, you'll make a lasting impression and increase the likelihood that your ideas will gain traction.

Share the Stage

Audiences find monologues boring. Thanks to advances in entertainment, they've become accustomed to quick action, rapid scene changes, intense visual stimulation, and soundtracks that make the heart race. They're no longer willing to sit attentively for an hour while a single speaker drones on.

The key to getting and holding their attention is having new things continually happen. You can do that by:

- **Bringing in other presenters:** Invite others to join you on the stage or by video. Consider which experts or analysts in your organization or industry would add meat and credibility to your presentation. And look for ways your team members can play to their strengths. If your colleague Sam is quick on his feet, for example, have him lead the Q&A.

- **Mixing up your media:** Try alternating between slides and other media. Hang posters and exhibits on the wall, place tchotchkes on the table that tie into the theme of your talk, or have a helper unveil a prop or new product while you speak. Add video to inject humor, boost credibility through testimonials, or clarify concepts with animated infographics. If you're talking about a product, demo it—hold it, display it, allow people to interact with it. If you're explaining a concept, try drawing on a flipchart or a whiteboard—it varies the pace and audiences often find it endearing because it makes all but the most artistic presenters vulnerable and thus accessible. Or you can hire a graphic recorder to capture your message visually on a large strip of butcher paper while you talk. She can synthesize what's being said in real time, creating a mural that memorializes the talk. Display it somewhere prominent in your department as a reminder of the goals everyone agreed on at the last vision meeting.

You can reengage your audience several times during your talk by alternating presenters and changing up your media. Of course, all those moving parts require planning and rehearsal—but they'll also keep people tuned in.

Section 5
Slides

At our studio we don't write our stories,
we draw them.

—**Walt Disney**

Think Like a Designer

To make the point that design thinking goes "hand-in-hand with financial success" in business, *Fast Company* cited an intriguing Design Council study in its October 2007 letter from the editor: "A portfolio of 63 design-driven British companies . . . trounced the FTSE 100 index over 13 years."

A chart like the one in figure 5-1 accompanied the letter. What does this have to do with presentations? A lot.

Presentations are one of the most popular business communication tools, second only to e-mail. They attract clients and keep employees on track. And the most effective presenters think like designers. Good presenters display data clearly, simply, and compellingly, as in the chart in figure 5-1. They select visuals that convey meaning and brand value. They create and arrange slides that persuade audiences and help them solve problems.

After reading the tips in the Slides section of this guide, you won't be a master designer—but you'll make better choices when confronted by the empty expanse of a virgin slide.

FIGURE 5-1

Design contributes to the bottom line

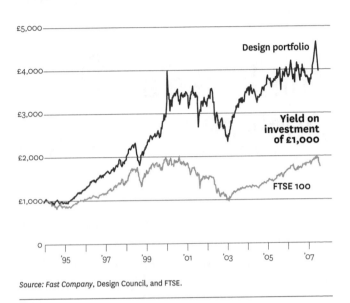

Source: *Fast Company*, Design Council, and FTSE.

Create Slides People Can "Get" in Three Seconds

Audiences can process only one stream of information at a time. They'll either listen to you speak or read your slides—they won't do both simultaneously (not without missing key parts of your message, anyway). So make sure they can quickly comprehend your visuals and then turn their attention back to what you're saying.

Let's say you're using the default template in Power-Point, and you completely fill in the field that says "Click to Add Text" each time you create a slide. That field holds about 80 words, and the average reading speed is 250 words per minute. So, if you develop 40 text-heavy slides for a 40-minute presentation, people will miss about 13 minutes (one-third!) of your talk just because they're too busy reading your slides to listen.

Another important reason to keep your slides simple: Research shows that people learn more effectively from multimedia messages when they're stripped of extraneous words, graphics, animation, and sounds. The extras actually *take away* meaning because they become a distraction. They overtax the audience's cognitive resources.

Each slide should pass what I call the *glance test*: People should be able to comprehend it in three seconds. Think of your slides as billboards. When people drive, they only briefly take their eyes off their main focus—the road—to process billboard information. Similarly, your audience should focus intently on what you're saying, looking only briefly at your slides when you display them.

To create slides that pass the glance test:

- **Start with a clean surface:** Instead of using the default "Click to Add Title" and "Click to Add Text" slide master, turn off all the master prompts and start with a blank slide. And when you add elements, make sure you have a good reason. Does the audience need to see your logo on each slide to remember who you work for? Does that blue swoosh add meaning? If not, leave it off.

- **Limit your text:** Keep the text short and easy to skim. Scale the type as large as possible so the people in the back of the room can see it.

- **Coordinate visual elements:** Select one typeface—two at most—for the entire slide deck. Use a consistent color palette throughout (limit yourself to three complementary colors, plus a couple of neutral shades, like gray or pale blue). Photos should be taken by the same photographer or look as if they are. Illustrations should be done in the same style.

- **Arrange elements with care:** When you project your slides, they'll be many times larger than they are on your laptop screen—so they need to be tidy. (Blown up, unkempt slides look downright chaotic.) Align your graphics and text blocks. Size objects appropriately. If one element is larger than another, the audience will interpret that to mean the larger object is more important.

Take a look at the "before" slide (figure 5-2). It fails the glance test because it's packed with text.

But when you streamline the text and incorporate simple visual elements—as in figure 5-3—you help the audience process the information much more quickly.

Presentation software gives us many shiny, seductive elements to work with. But there's beauty and clarity in

FIGURE 5-2

Before

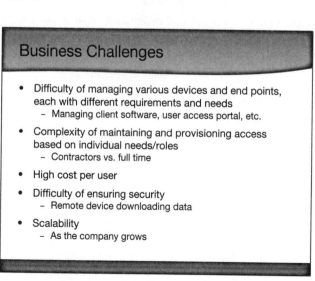

FIGURE 5-3

After

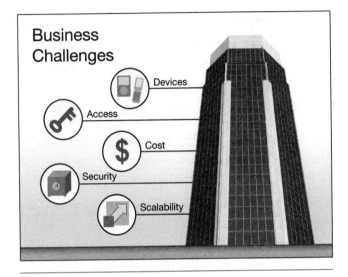

restraint. Though you can develop your visual sensibility by studying well-designed publications, you may also want to ask a professional designer to customize a template for you so you'll have a solid foundation to build from.

Choose the Right Type of Slide

If you're feeling overwhelmed by endless possibilities as you're creating slides, rest assured—all slides can be boiled down to the following types. Here's how they work, and when you'll use them.

Walk-in slide

This slide is already up when people enter the room. It creates the first impression. You may want it to display your company's branding, for example, or an image that sets the tone for your presentation.

Title slide

Here's where you show the title of your talk and (if you're addressing an external crowd) your name, title, and company. Include a title slide even if you don't state the title when you speak; it helps orient and focus the audience.

Navigation slide

This type of slide helps the audience see where you are in the presentation. You can, for example, show section

FIGURE 5-4

Navigation slide

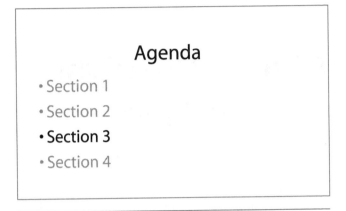

titles as you move from point to point or periodically show an agenda slide that highlights where you are in your talk (see figure 5-4).

Bullet slide

Use bullets to cluster related ideas into a list, but don't display them all at once. If you do, your audience will get ahead of you—and get bored. Instead, control your pacing with a "build" (have each bullet appear as you cover it by animating each one). If the bullets on your slide don't have to be associated together, give each point its own slide.

Big-word slide

This type of slide shows a single word or short phrase in large type—the one message or idea you want to convey at that moment. Sometimes I use a single word to set up a visual surprise on the next slide. When I was speaking at a high-tech company's annual sales meeting, for instance, I told a story about my first sales job: selling candy for the Camp Fire Girls as a kid. I had clipped a newspaper photo of my troop with a trophy for selling the most candy—but I wanted that part to be a surprise. So first, I slipped in a slide that said, "Victory is sweet." This text not only explained an important reason *why* people sell but also teed up the photo showing our goofy fifth-grade smiles and our skinny arms holding up a trophy that was bigger than we were.

Quote slide

Project quotes by experts or from important documents to add credibility or factual support to your message, but clearly show where the material came from. Use quotation marks and include a source line. Project only one quote at a time—more than one will muddy the focus. And try not to exceed 30 words. That allows you to fit in attribution without sacrificing readability. You can also borrow a technique that I've seen several TED presenters use effectively: Supplement the visual with a recording of the person you're quoting or (if that's not available) add voice-over so the audience feels as if it's reading along with the author of the quote.

Data slide

You may need to display data when explaining your research, for example, or reporting on your business unit's performance, or making a controversial argument that requires proof. Be judicious, though, so you don't overwhelm people with numbers they don't really need to know. Visually emphasize what part of the data you want people to look at by rendering everything else in the chart in gray (see "Clarify the Data" later in this section of the guide).

Diagram slide

Diagrams translate abstract, invisible concepts into something people can see. Use them to show connections between ideas or to illustrate processes. You may want to transform some of your bullet slides into diagrams to clarify the type of relationship your points and subpoints have with each other (see "Turn Words into Diagrams" later in this section).

Conceptual image slide

Sometimes showing is more powerful than telling. Project photos or illustrations to convey concepts or even

FIGURE 5-5

Conceptual image slide

combine them. Slaveryfootprint.org used the familiar image of a clothing tag with provocative wording to open consumers' eyes to the realities of slave labor in supply chains (figure 5-5).

Video slide

A video slide provides a nice break from a series of static slides. Use videos of talking heads to endorse your concept, for example, or animated infographics to explain it. Many images from stock photography houses also come in video versions.

Walk-out slide

Leave people with something useful as they exit the room. You may want to re-project a rousing call to action, show your contact information, or display a nicely branded slide and play music that reinforces the mood you've created.

Storyboard One Idea per Slide

Filmmakers sketch out their shots *before* production begins to make sure they'll hang together structurally, conceptually, and visually. Good presenters use a similar planning process before they sweat over their slides.

Sure, you're not Steven Spielberg, but don't be intimidated. Basic storyboarding isn't hard, and it saves you more time than it takes.

When you're storyboarding a presentation:

- **Keep it simple:** Draw small visual representations of your ideas on 1.5″ × 2″ sticky notes (see figure 5-6). Constraining your ideas to a small sketch space forces you to use simple, clear words and pictures as proof of concept before creating slides in presentation software. Don't be embarrassed by rudimentary sketches. This is an ideation phase; doodles work fine as long as you understand them (and if you don't, the concept is probably too complex anyway).

FIGURE 5-6

Use stickies to keep it simple

- **Limit yourself to one idea per slide:** There's no reason to crowd several ideas onto one slide. Slides are free. Make as many as you need to give each idea its own moment onstage (as in figure 5-7).

The sketching process helps you clarify what you want to say and how you want to say it. As Dan Roam, author of *The Back of the Napkin*, points out, "All the real problems of today are multidimensional. . . . There is no way to fully understand them—thus no way to effectively begin solving them—without at some point literally drawing them out."

FIGURE 5-7

One idea per slide

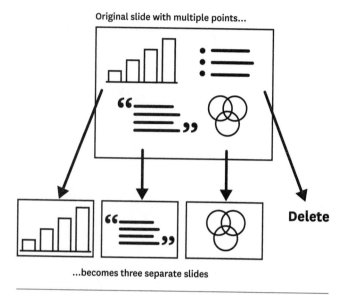

Original slide with multiple points...

...becomes three separate slides

As you storyboard, you'll be able to tell immediately which concepts are clunky or overly complex (you'll run out of space on your sticky notes). Eliminate them, and brainstorm new ways to communicate those messages.

Chances are good you can develop at least a couple of your storyboarding doodles into graphics or diagrams you'll actually use in the presentation. If they'll help the audience understand or remember your verbal message, they're worth including. But even if you don't display any images when you present, nice big type on the screen is better than dense prose.

Avoid Visual Clichés

When your CFO announces at an all-staff meeting that the company's financials are "right on target," does he treat you and your colleagues to the all-too-familiar image of a bull's-eye?

Nothing gets eyes a-glazing like a visual cliché. If you want your presentation to stand out (in a good way) from the others your audience has seen, throw out the first visual concepts that come to mind. They're the ones that occur to everyone else, too. Brainstorm several ideas for

TABLE 5-1

Find new visual metaphors

Concept	Cliché	Unique
Goal	Bull's-eye	Maze; threshold
Partnership	Handshake in front of globe	Reef ecosystem; Fred Astaire and Ginger Rogers
Security	Lock and key	Doberman pinscher; pepper spray

each concept you want to illustrate—and you'll work your way toward fresh, surprising images.

Table 5-1 gives some examples of visual clichés and more-creative ways to illustrate the same concepts.

Arrange Slide Elements with Care

By carefully arranging your slide elements, you can help your audience process the information more easily—and that, as we've discussed, frees up people to hear what you're saying.

Follow these five design principles when arranging elements to simplify your slides.

Flow

Placement governs flow—that is, how the eye travels across a space. You can direct people's eyes to certain areas of a slide and help your audience get to the important points quickly. People should be able to move their eyes across your slide in one back-and-forth motion and be done processing the information.

In figure 5-8, your eye takes in the cluster of grapes, then moves to the text, then focuses on one individual grape.

FIGURE 5-8

Flow—Part 1

The next example (figure 5-9) shows one of a series of five points made. Your eye moves from left to right: You see the number 5 and the title, then your eye follows the path to the ridgeline.

Contrast

Our eyes are drawn to things that stand out, so designers use contrast to focus attention. Create contrast through your elements' size, shape, color, and proximity.

Look at figure 5-10, where the presenter compared cross-sections of skin and soil to show that tending to both requires an understanding of the microbiological activity beneath the surface. Notice how the blurred

FIGURE 5-9

Flow—Part 2

FIGURE 5-10

Contrast

background images set off the stark white illustrations in high relief so they can be processed quickly.

White space

White space is the open space surrounding items of interest. Presenters are often tempted to fill it up with additional content that competes for attention. But including a healthy amount of white space imparts a feeling of luxury (advertisers have discovered that it creates higher perceived value) and sharpens viewers' focus by isolating elements.

That doesn't necessarily mean that everything is literally "white"—just that the design feels spacious. See the example in figure 5-11:

FIGURE 5-11

White space

"Products are made in the factory, but brands are created in the mind."

Walter Landor
Founder of Landor Associates

If we'd paired the quote with a larger or more detailed image, your eye wouldn't know where to begin. Buried, the quote's message would have lost its power.

Hierarchy

A clear visual hierarchy allows viewers to quickly ascertain a slide's most important elements.

The sample slide in figure 5-12, citing a statistic from a recent McKinsey study, has a top-down hierarchy: You process the picture, and then the large percentage, and then the supporting copy.

Unity

Slides with visual unity look as though the same person created them and make your message feel cohesive. You

FIGURE 5-12

Hierarchy

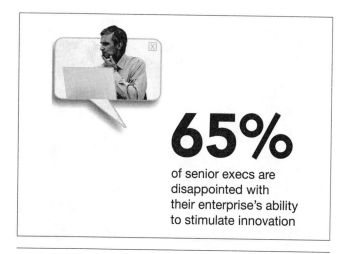

65%
of senior execs are
disappointed with
their enterprise's ability
to stimulate innovation

FIGURE 5-13

Unity—Part 1

FIGURE 5-14

Unity—Part 2

can achieve this through consistent type styles, color, image treatment, and element placement throughout the slide deck.

The slides in figures 5-13 and 5-14 feel united for a couple of reasons: Both of their backgrounds are dark around the edges and lighter in the middle. Also, all the type and the images are black.

Clarify the Data

When displaying data in a presentation, pursue clarity above all else. The people in your audience can't spend extra time with your projected charts or pull them closer to examine them, as they do with charts in print. They have to get meaning from your numbers at a distance, before you click away.

People will interpret your data slides first by reading the titles, then by looking at the shapes the data make, and then by reading the axes. It's a multistep process, complex to begin with. So if the information you're displaying is *visually complex*, the audience won't have time to comprehend it.

These rules of thumb will help you clarify—and simplify—your data.

Highlight what's important

Start by asking, "What would I like people to remember about the data?"—and give that point visual emphasis. If you're projecting a chart about sales trends over five years but talking specifically about how sales are consistently low in the first quarter, show the first-quarter bar of each year in a rich color and other bars in a neutral color, like gray. Deemphasize grid lines, borders, axes, and labels—you'll provide that kind of context when you speak, so your visuals don't have to—and use contrast (color, size, or position) to draw the viewer's eye to where the meaning is.

Notice in figure 5-15 (top) how the grid lines and borders all have the same weight as the data, so the eye doesn't know where to go first. But the bottom image— borderless, with muted axes and gridlines—takes viewers right to the point: They see immediately that revenue leveled off after a spike early in the year.

Tell the truth

This may seem obvious, but many presenters play fast and loose with their charts. If you don't have a z-axis in

FIGURE 5-15

Highlight what's important

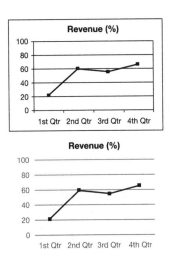

your data, omit 3-D effects—the depth can make your numbers look larger than they are. In a 3-D pie chart, for example, the pie piece in the foreground appears deceptively larger than the rest. Also, don't alter the proportions of your axes. Doing so can make a change in the numbers look more significant (figure 5-16a) or less so (figure 5-16b). Square grid lines (figure 5-16c) will keep your data true.

Pick the right chart for the job

The most common charts in business are pies, bars, matrixes, and line graphs. They serve different purposes, though. Use a line graph instead of a bar chart if the shape of the line will draw attention to your most impor-

FIGURE 5-16

Tell the truth

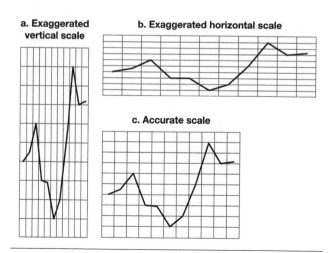

a. Exaggerated vertical scale

b. Exaggerated horizontal scale

c. Accurate scale

tant point. Use a matrix instead of multiple pie charts if you want to show relationships between the data points.

For example, the slide in figure 5-17 uses pie charts to show how airline ticket sales break down between three different sales channels: online, agents, and direct sales. But there's not much you can deduce from these charts, because they're visually similar.

Lay out the data in a matrix, however, and suddenly it's clear that total sales for Airline 3 are almost double the others (figure 5-18).

Sometimes the best chart is no chart at all. If a number conveys your key message most clearly on its own, show just that number—huge—on the slide.

FIGURE 5-17

The wrong chart for the job

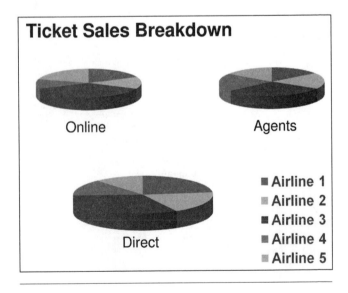

FIGURE 5-18

The right chart for the job

Ticket Sales Breakdown

	Airline 1	Airline 2	Airline 3	Airline 4	Airline 5
Online	20	15	40	12	22
Agents	15	18	30	20	15
Direct	25	20	35	15	12
Total	**60**	**53**	**105**	**47**	**49**

Find the narrative in the data

Explain not just the "what," but the "why" and the "how" of your data. Maybe the numbers went up, but what *made* them go up? What impact did people have on them? How will people be affected *by* them?

Use concrete comparisons to express magnitude

The bigger a number is, the tougher it is to grasp. Millions, billions, and trillions sound a lot alike, but they're nowhere near each other in magnitude. Help your audience understand scale by communicating large numbers in concrete terms. For example, if you're trying to get an audience to visualize a billion square feet, hold up a carpet square that's 12″ × 12″ and tell them it would take a billion of those squares to cover Manhattan.

Turn Words into Diagrams

Diagrams are great tools for illustrating relationships. They clarify concepts so an audience can see at a glance how parts of a whole work together. For example, if your organization is merging with two others, you can use a diagram of three overlapping circles to signify redundancies between departments. Or if you want to encourage your team members to innovate iteratively, try using a flow diagram that loops back on itself in several places to illustrate the process of working out kinks in a prototype.

When you're creating your presentation visuals, try turning some of your words into diagrams that *reinforce* your speech. It's easy to translate words into diagrams when you have a visual taxonomy at your disposal—and I'm providing one here.

Because my firm has visualized concepts for companies and brands for more than 20 years, my designers' notebooks are filled with great business diagrams. Looking for patterns, I clipped thousands of sketches from those notebooks and sorted them into the following commonly used (and universally understood) types of diagrams.

FIGURE 5-19

Types of diagrams

A Network

HUB AND
SPOKES

SPOKES

FLARE

RING

B Segment

DONUT

PIE

C Join

HOOK

OVERLAP

D Flow

LOOP

PARALLEL

LINEAR

MERGE
AND DIVIDE

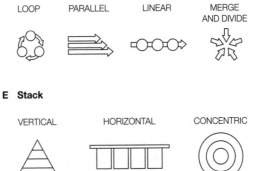

E Stack

VERTICAL

HORIZONTAL

CONCENTRIC

The diagrams in figure 5-19 illustrate these kinds of relationships:

- **Network**

  Example: A hub-and-spokes diagram can illustrate the stakeholders from various departments who come together to make an initiative successful.

- **Segment**

  Example: A donut can show how separate products fit into a suite of offerings.

- **Join**

  Example: A hook diagram can depict a relationship between supply chain partners.

- **Flow**

  Example: Parallel arrows can show two teams working in concert toward a goal.

- **Stack**

  Example: Vertical layers can illustrate discrete fiscal-year goals as building blocks that will lead to profitability.

So, how can you use these diagrams in your presentation? Look through your slides and find a list of bullets. Those bullets should "feel" related—that's why you grouped them together in the first place. Circle the verbs or nouns on the slide and consider *how* they're related.

That relationship will most likely fall into one of the categories in figure 5-19. Now see if you can use one of the diagrams in that category to replace your bullet slide. Repeat the process with other text slides.

Consider two sets of slides (figures 5-20a and 5-20b; figures 5-21a and 5-21b) showing how a list of bullet points ("Before") can be turned into a diagram ("After").

The taxonomy in figure 5-19 isn't exhaustive, and there's room for creativity within each category. You can use different shapes and styles for the nodes and connectors, and so on (go to diagrammer.com for thousands of choices). But it covers most of the bases, so it takes some of the pressure off as you're working to meet your deadline.

FIGURE 5-20a

Before

We follow the same basic process every time

- We start with the invention. We take early stage ideas and turn them into demos—not technical demos but conceptual ones, like the rough version of Flare you saw.

- Then our team takes this seed of an idea to customers, in conferences and forums, to get feedback that helps us shape it into something even more useful.

- We improve it and build a prototype that we give to a set of early adopters, who use it and give us more feedback.

- Eventually, after a few quick cycles of this process, we standardize the product features.

- Only then is it ready to go out to our larger group of customers, like the finished version of Flare you saw.

FIGURE 5-20b

After

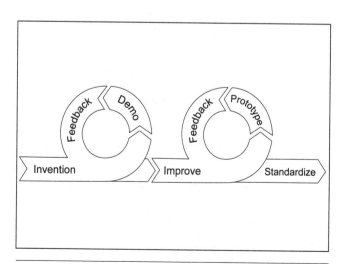

FIGURE 5-21a

Before

Research Programs

Concentrate on four research programs

- Domestic Energy Development
- Environmental Technologies
- Carbon Management
- Energy Efficiency

The potential impact of all of our programs will extend beyond policy makers to corporations and citizens around the world.

FIGURE 5-21b

After

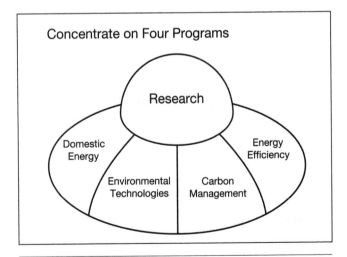

Concentrate on Four Programs

Research

Domestic Energy

Energy Efficiency

Environmental Technologies

Carbon Management

Use the Right Number of Slides

How many slides should you have? That depends on your audience, the technology you're using, the setting you're in, your own sense of pacing, and how comfortable you are with a clicker. Some presenters could spend an hour on three slides; others could go through 200 or more and you'd never know it.

Consider these slide-count variables as you're creating your presentation.

No slides

If you need to make a very personal connection with your audience or you're delivering a short talk in a casual environment, go without slides. They don't work in every situation. As Andrew Dlugan says in his "Six Minutes" blog about public speaking, presenters shouldn't use slides in a commencement speech, a eulogy, a wedding toast, or a layoff announcement. If you're unsure whether they're appropriate, bring them with you but also carry a printout of your slide notes in case you decide when you arrive that it's best to leave your laptop off.

Moderate slide count

Some experts recommend 1 to 2 slides per minute, or 30 to 60 slides for an hour-long talk. That's about the average count in corporate presentations—but most of them cram too much information on each slide. If you've broken your content down to one idea per slide (see "Storyboard One Idea per Slide" earlier in the Slides section), you may end up with more than 60.

High slide count

Some presenters use 5 slides per minute. This rapid-fire style keeps the audience extra alert because people will visually reengage with each click—but it requires a lot of rehearsal and careful pacing. In a 40-minute talk, I typically use 145 slides. (If you count "builds" within each slide—where I reveal bullets one at a time, and so forth—I click up to 300 times.) But when I ask audiences how many slides they think I used, they usually say between 30 and 50.

Social media slide count

The most popular presentations on social media sites like slideshare.com have more than 75 slides that you can read in 2 to 3 minutes. They also tend to be built like children's books—sentence, visual, sentence, visual—to facilitate quick clicking.

Don't worry about slide count. Just make your *slides* count.

Know When to Animate

When things move, eyes are drawn to them. So animation is a powerful communication tool—but only when applied judiciously and in a way that enhances your message.

It's tempting to include every feature and flashy effect that's available—but that would be like adding rhinestones to every outfit in your closet. You'd be blinded by all the bling when you opened the door, and you wouldn't know what to pick.

Effective animation:

- **Shows how things work:** Use animation and motion to control eye movement as you reveal how things are put together, explain changes, show direction, or illustrate sequence. If, for example, you've got a stack of boxes showing how parts of your software application fit together, you can provide information on one part at a time, without crowding the visual: When you click on a box, have a "drawer" slide out from behind it to reveal details.

- **Creates contrast:** Show many slides with no animation so that when you do use it, it stands out.

- **Looks natural:** Just like actors on a stage, elements can enter your slide, interact, and then leave the scene. But the movement should seem natural and controlled, not busy and frenetic.

- **Does not annoy:** Most content isn't any clearer if you make it spin, twitch, or twirl. Gratuitous features like these just get on people's nerves, so don't waste time on them.

Section 6
Delivery

Golden Rule: Never deliver a presentation you wouldn't want to sit through.

—**Motto at Duarte, Inc.**

Rehearse Your Material Well

There's no such thing as overrehearsing your delivery. Not that you should memorize your talk—if you do, you'll come across as stiff and struggle to connect with the audience. But know your material inside and out. That way, you can adapt more easily if the environment, audience, or technology suddenly changes on you (something often does). Also, audiences can tell if you try to wing it—and they feel slighted. It sends the message that you don't value them or their time. Perhaps most important, rehearsing frees you up to be more *present* in your talk and fully engage with the people in front of you.

When you rehearse, leave plenty of time to:

- **Get honest feedback from a skilled presenter:** As the presenter, you're so familiar with (and probably attached to) your ideas that you may think you're making each point more clearly and persuasively than you are. So ask a skilled presenter to give you honest feedback. Give her a printout of your slides and have her jot down what you say well, what you don't, what's essential to keep, and what's distracting. She might say things like: "When you put it that way, people won't follow you," and "That term sounds derogatory to me," and "I thought you expressed it better last time, when you said . . ." The extra set of eyes and ears helps you see and hear yourself as the audience will.

- **Prepare a short version:** Many variables in a presentation can go wrong, leaving you with less time than you expected. The technology doesn't always work. Other speakers might cut into your time slot by running long. An impatient executive may interrupt you with lots of questions. Prepare a presentation that fits your scheduled time, but also craft and rehearse a version that's much shorter, just in case.

- **Fiddle with your slides:** Continue to tweak your slides until the day you present. Refining a bit of text here and adding an image there is a form of rehearsal. You become more deeply familiar with the content as you engage with your slides—so when you present, they feel seamlessly integrated with your message, not tacked-on or disruptive.

- **Rehearse a few times in slide-show mode:** Because slide-show mode doesn't allow you to peek at the notes view, it forces you into an even greater familiarity with the material and allows you to focus on pacing and visualize the flow. Look for choppy transitions from slide to slide, inconsistent graphics, and awkward builds as you reveal new bullets, so you can smooth things out.

- **Practice on camera:** Record some of your final rehearsals on video. You don't need a professional setup. Use a webcam or the camera on your cell phone or tablet. Pretend you are in front of an audience, and address the camera as if it's a person. When you're done, review the video to assess not just your content but also your stage presence, eye contact, facial expressions, gestures, and ease of movement. Identify where you don't appear natural, relaxed, or in command of your material—and work on those areas.

Know the Venue and Schedule

Scoping out the room in advance will help you navigate it. If you can't check it out in person, look for details online or ask the host to describe it. Sometimes, if you get this information early enough, you can change the setup to meet your preferences. If you're leading an off-site meeting for a team of six, for example, and you've been assigned a large conference space, see if you can get a cozier room—or at least a smaller table to encourage discussion.

Don't make any assumptions about the space. When I was invited to speak to 70 people at Google, in my head I pictured rows of chairs. But when I got there, I was taken to a tiny conference room with 20 people crammed in—and 50 small faces of webcam participants projected on the wall. If I'd known what the room would be like, I would have prepared to facilitate a conversation instead of delivering a formal presentation. Instead, I found myself making lots of last-minute mental adjustments, like figuring out where to stand and where to focus my eye contact, and that threw me off my stride.

Avoid such surprises by getting information about:

- **Floor and seating plan:** How is the room arranged? Does it have classroom seating? Round tables? Is the size of the room appropriate for the number of attendees you expect? It's better for people to sit close together, feeding off one another's energy, than to feel lost and disconnected in a cavernous space. Will you be elevated on a stage? Will the audience be able to see you if you stand on the same level as everyone else to make your talk feel less like a lecture? Do you have room to walk around and connect with people? If you'll be on stage, where will the lights hit the floor? Mark any pockets of darkness with tape so you can avoid them (important for talks recorded on video). Does the room have any poles that will obstruct the audience's view? Do what you can to work around them. Is there a podium? Remove it—it's a visual barrier that puts distance between you and the audience—unless you need a place to put your notes.

- **Food plan:** Are you presenting near a mealtime? Find out whether food will be provided. If not, build in time for people—including yourself—to grab a bite. Or if you're presenting within your organization, bring some snacks. A hungry audience won't focus on your message. Will you be speaking during a sit-down meal? You'll need adequate amplification so people can hear you above the sounds of forks and knives. Or see if you can wait until the food service crew clears the dishes before you speak.

- **Show flow:** What will the order of events be? Check with the organizer. Will you be introduced, or do you need to prepare your own introduction? Who will speak before you and after you? What messages will others present? It's nice to reference things others are saying. If you're toward the end of a long list of speakers, keep your message short and simple—the audience will already be tired and overloaded with information. And if you're following a presenter with a contrary view, you can prepare to address any seeds of resistance he might plant in the audience. Speaking at a conference? Look at sessions in the same time slot as yours to find out if you'll be competing with a popular workshop, for example, or a famous author doing a book signing. That'll help you gauge whether the room will fill up.

- **Recording:** Will your talk be recorded? If so, locate the cameras and look at them often to connect with remote viewers or listeners. Do you want to restrict distribution of your recorded presentation? Make that clear to the organizers. Once, when I spoke to a group of 250 professional women about overcoming obstacles, I knew I was being recorded but thought only attendees could access the recording, via a password-protected website. A local TV channel ended up broadcasting my entire presentation. My talk was very raw. I wouldn't have gotten so personal if I'd known it would go beyond the room.

Anticipate Technology Glitches

Equipment often malfunctions—even for people who aren't as technologically challenged as I am. So arrange a tech walkthrough or, if that's not possible, give yourself *at least* 30 minutes to set up.

Here's a checklist I've developed after years of trial by fire to avoid last-minute frenzy from tech glitches:

- **Get to know the AV person:** Learn his name and treat him well. He'll work extra hard and extra fast for you if he likes you.

- **Test all the equipment:** Do a dry run using the projector, the clicker, and any audio equipment beforehand. Make sure it all works.

- **Bring backups:** If a piece of technology is critical to the success of your talk, request that it be provided—but also bring your own. That goes for the projector, the cables needed to connect it, the clicker, and any audio equipment you'll need. I travel with my own speakers because at-venue audio often doesn't work. Venture capitalist and former Apple marketer Guy Kawasaki even brings his own in-ear microphone when he presents. Also, back up the content of your presentation on drives and in the cloud—and make printouts of your slides and notes.

- **Prerecord your demos:** If you're planning to demonstrate software, an app, or a website, have a recorded version of your demo on your machine in case the Internet connection is slow or down at the time of your talk.

- **Test your slide deck:** Click through every single slide. This is your last time to see what the slides look like projected in the room. You want to confirm that you've grabbed the right version, that everything is legible from the back of the room, and that each time you click, the slides advance to the right content. Sometimes the distance between the clicker and the computer backstage is too far for the signal to reach, and the AV team has to make adjustments.

- **Try out the comfort monitors:** Confirm that your comfort monitors (teleprompters) work and you can read from them. At a technical walkthrough the day before a presentation, I discovered that my comfort monitors were so small I couldn't read anything from the stage. I wanted to use monitors rather than rely solely on printouts because I'd be quoting lengthy excerpts from famous speeches. So that night, I doubled the font size and saved myself a lot of embarrassment.

- **Play all media:** When transferring files to a venue's machines, it's easy to forget to grab video and audio files. Double-check that you have all your media in one folder and that the file types will play on the machines you'll be using.

- **Confirm type of projection:** Check the screen's aspect ratio (usually 16:9 or 4:3), and make sure your slides are the right dimensions. Also consider whether they'll be front- or rear-projected— and mark the floor with tape so you won't walk through the light beam and have slides projected across your face when you're speaking.

- **Find out if people will attend remotely:** The odds of technical mishaps go way up in remote presentations—especially ones that involve last-minute equipment changes. Once I tested all my videos before walking onstage, only to discover moments before I began speaking that the AV crew switched machines to accommodate a large remote group. The crew forgot to copy over my video files—so I did my best to describe what people *would have seen* if we had those files.

Manage Your Stage Fright

Before you present, does your heart speed up? Do you sweat? Does your mouth go dry and your breathing become erratic? That's your fight-or-flight instinct kicking in. Your body is telling you to flee because your brain perceives the audience as a possible threat: People might judge, challenge, or resist you.

You may also fear the fact that presentation delivery can't be undone. It's live, and it's final.

A little bit of fear can be a good thing. I actually do a better job of presenting when I'm mildly nervous—it's like a shot of adrenaline. But don't let it overwhelm you.

Here are a few ways to manage your stage fright before you present:

- **Quiet your mind:** Stop the self-critical internal chatter and think instead about something that calms you. Take a short walk outside. Listen to soothing music.

- **Breathe:** Sit on a chair or the floor, breathe deeply, and hold it in. Then take in one more gasp of air to fill your lungs even more—and let it all out very slowly. By doing this four times in a row, I can calm my body down in less than a minute.

- **Laugh:** Read your favorite humor website or watch a funny video. Laughing doesn't just distract you from your fear—it releases tension.

- **Visualize:** Communication coach Nick Morgan, the author of *Trust Me*, suggests my favorite fear-busting technique: "Role-play in your mind a communication between you and your favorite person. . . . Form a memory of what that feels like physically, not about what you say. Notice everything you can about your behavior. . . .What are you doing with your hands? . . . How close are you? . . . Catalogue and remember the behavior, and then use that behavior."

- **Remember your audience's flaws:** You've spent time thinking about how the people in your audience might resist your message—and rightly so. They do have that power. But, having studied them, you should also have insights into what makes *them* human and frail. Remembering that they're just as flawed as you are will help calm your nerves.

Set the Right Tone for Your Talk

Your audience will size you up before you utter a word—so it's critical to make a positive, message-appropriate first impression.

What's the first thing you want people to think or experience? What mood do you want to create? Set the right tone for your talk by attending to the following details.

Precommunication

When you invite others to your presentation, send a thoughtfully written agenda with a concise but telling subject line—and be explicit about what the audience will get out of it. All communication leading up to your talk will affect your credibility and impact—so put as much thought and care into it as into the presentation itself. (See "Persuade Beyond the Stage" in the Media section.)

Atmosphere

Special touches in the room let people know what to expect and prime them for the type of experience you want them to have. If you're giving a calculated, chilling speech, a cold, sparsely appointed room works. Use bright lighting for a casual talk; go a bit darker for a formal one. Provide refreshments (even for small, familiar groups) to make people feel welcome. Music, props, and projected images can also help set the tone.

Appearance

As much as you want the audience to like you for your mind, people will make quick judgments based on your appearance. Suit up to address potential clients, for example, or investors. Dress more casually when introducing yourself to a new group of direct reports, to signal that you're accessible. In *Enchantment: The Art of Changing Hearts, Minds, and Actions*, Guy Kawasaki suggests matching your audience (or dressing for a "tie"). If you underdress, you're saying, "I don't respect you"; and if you overdress, you're saying, "I'm better than you."

Disposition

The moment people see you, your disposition should prepare them for your message. For your content to ring true, do you need to come across as passionate? Humbled by the challenges ahead? If you're announcing a layoff, be somber, not smiley. If your talk is upbeat, chat with individuals as the group gathers; shake hands if you're meeting for the first time. No matter what tone you're trying to establish, be available and sincere.

Be Yourself

Transparency wins people over. Though you'll want to come across as smart and articulate, it's even more important to be open and sincere so people will trust you and your ideas.

It's OK if you're nervous. Audiences are gracious. As business communication expert Victoria Labalme points out, they'll "forgive a stumble, an 'um,' or a section where you backtrack as long as they know that your heart is in the right place."

She adds: "Your audience wants you to be real. So avoid sounding like a corporate spokesperson—but don't portray false humility, either. Playing small and meek when inside you know (and the audience knows) you're a giant will not win you any fans. Authenticity means claiming who you are."

If you love what you do, for instance, let your enthusiasm show.

Microsoft CEO Steve Ballmer explodes with so much passion when he presents that his sweaty, breathless dancing became a YouTube phenomenon (figure 6-1).

FIGURE 6-1

Steve Ballmer's famous "monkey boy" dance

In a January 2012 article about Ballmer, *Business-Week* mused, "He plays the cheerleader in public appearances in an apparent effort to prove that no one can top his love of Microsoft—and he succeeds cringingly well." It's over-the-top, but it's all him. No one questions his authenticity, and the man can rally his troops.

And then there's Susan Cain, who took the opposite tack when she gave one of the most buzzed-about talks at TED 2012. Cain spoke quietly and convincingly about being an introvert in a world that rewards extroverts. Her style suited her—and her subject matter—perfectly. She seemed comfortable onstage, but she certainly wasn't dramatic or even passionate. That wouldn't have been natural, given her personality and her topic. Instead, she delivered her message in a way that would resonate with fellow introverts: "The world needs you, and it needs the things you carry. So I wish you the best of all possible journeys and the courage to speak softly."

Communicate with Your Body

People will read your body language to decide if they can trust you and your expertise. Constricted and contrived gestures will make you seem insecure. Larger movement conveys confidence and openness.

Use your physical expression to its fullest with the following techniques:

- **Project emotion with your face:** Connect with the audience by using your face to convey your feelings. Smile, laugh, open your mouth in disbelief. Before you begin your talk, try moving every facial muscle you can—it'll help you warm up.

- **Peel yourself away from your slides:** If you turn your back to the audience to look at your slides, you put up a barrier. As much as you can, keep your eyes on the people who have come to hear you.

- **Open up your posture:** Avoid a "closed" stance, such as folding your arms, standing with legs crossed, putting your hands in your pockets, or clasping your hands behind or in front of you. It signals discomfort.

- **Exaggerate your movements:** Fill the space around you, especially if you're speaking in a large room. Use the same types of gestures you would if you were having a personal conversation—but make them bigger and more deliberate. Before your presentation, stretch your arms as wide as you can and as tall as you can (even stand on your toes). This helps you open up your chest cavity and practice exaggerating your gestures.

- **Match gestures with content:** Gestures should complement or amplify what you're saying. If you're presenting a record year in sales, go "big" with your arms and your smile. If your team barely missed its targets, bring everything in, perhaps showing a tiny little gap between your thumb and forefinger.

Brain scientist Jill Bolte Taylor coordinated her gestures and content beautifully when she described in her 2008 TED talk what it was like to have a massive stroke. She threw her arms upward to convey the unexpected rush of euphoria she'd felt as the left side of her brain shut down (figure 6-2a); she brought them back down when she described how she'd surrendered her spirit, ready to transition out of this world (figure 6-2b).

When you tape yourself in rehearsal, you may identify gestures, movements, or facial expressions that look

FIGURE 6-2a

Jill Bolte Taylor, arms up

FIGURE 6-2b

Jill Bolte Taylor, arms down

lackluster or unnatural. Re-create those gestures so you can physically feel them, and then practice new ones that would be appropriate replacements. As with golf, focus on how it feels as you do it so you can create "muscle memory" of what works.

Communicate with Your Voice

Your voice is multitalented. It can sound:

- **Assertive:** Firm, unyielding, significant, focused

- **Cautious:** Measured, enunciated, understated

- **Critical:** Harsh, angry, upset, pointed, caustic

- **Humorous:** Comedic, light, novel, irreverent

- **Motivational:** Uplifting, encouraging, friendly

- **Sympathetic:** Emotional, moving, personal, delicate

- **Neutral:** Casual, technical, dispassionate, informative

And it does all this through pitch, tone, volume, pacing, and enunciation.

Many business presenters have a dispassionate vocal style, assuming that it makes them sound objective or authoritative. But a flat delivery will bore your audience.

Instead, create contrast—and emphasis—through vocal variation. You can do this on your own or by tag-teaming with someone else. When my husband and I copresent our company's vision each year, our contrasting styles come through: He's soft-spoken and charmingly funny, whereas I'm dramatic and passionate. That mix works well for our content. He gets everyone to reflect on the firm's success, and I talk about the future with bold enthusiasm.

To ensure that your content comes through clearly, identify and remove verbal tics. Because silence makes most speakers uncomfortable, they tend to use words such as "um," "uh," "you know," "like," and "anyway" to fill up space between points. They'd almost always be better served by a pause, which gives the audience a chance to reflect.

I didn't think I had any verbal tics until I watched myself on video. After each key point, I said, "Right?" with an annoying lilt in my tone. It didn't take me long to remove that from my repertoire. I watched the video several times to cement it in my mind. At my very next speaking gig, I said it. Once. This word I didn't even know I used suddenly sounded like fingernails on a chalkboard. I caught myself two more times about to say it—and stopped. Becoming self-aware and really hearing how bad it sounded helped me correct myself in the moment.

Make Your Stories Come to Life

The beauty of an honest story—whether comedic or dramatic—is that it touches people. (See the Story section for details on how to apply storytelling principles when crafting and structuring your content.) But even the most compelling stories lose their power if they're not told well. How do you make yours come to life? Try the following two tips from business communication expert Victoria Labalme.

Reexperience your stories

Broadway actors relive stories each time they perform. It's how they keep their material fresh and engage audiences show after show. You can do the same. If you're talking about the time you got lost in a strange city at night to make a point about finding your way when there's no one around to guide you, re-create that scene. Don't be melodramatic or ridiculous. But narrate the story as if you're still in the moment, and you'll increase its impact on your audience. Use evocative, descriptive words. Enhance them with your stance and gestures.

One CEO reenacts the moment when his CFO came into his office and recommended that they not invest in subprime mortgages. The story is riveting partly because audiences know, in hindsight, how high the stakes were—but also because the CEO brings people *into* the scene. He describes the wood-paneled room, the view out the window on a clear day, and the moment of his razor's-edge decision—a decision that ultimately saved the company hundreds of millions of dollars. He then acknowledges his CFO for his sage advice at this critical juncture.

Rarely does someone approach a speaker weeks after a presentation to say, "I loved your third point on leadership." What people do say, however, is "I still think of the story you told . . ."

Use sensory details to set the scene

The more you can invoke the senses when telling a story, the better. Paint a visual picture, or the audience is left with a blank canvas. Also describe sounds, tastes, smells, and how things feel to the touch. "I waited in a chilly, mildewed alcove the size of an elevator" says a lot more than "I waited in a small room." By grounding yourself in such details, you'll avoid flowery, empty language reminiscent of greeting cards and embroidery pillows. You'll give your stories credibility and staying power.

Work Effectively with Your Interpreter

As companies do business farther and farther from home, presenters increasingly need translation. And working with an interpreter always complicates things. You can make it easier, though, with preparation.

Start by picking the right type of interpreter for your situation. Three types are available:

- **Simultaneous:** The interpreter sits in a soundproof booth while you present without disruption. Audience members who need translation wear earphones. When I spoke to a large group of business leaders in Taiwan, more than half the audience used earphones. As a result, I got through a lot of material with little time lost. Simultaneous interpretation requires more overhead than the other types do, since it involves technology.

- **Consecutive:** The interpreter shares the stage with you. After you make a point, you pause for her to relay what you've said. You can use this approach in less-formal settings or if you don't have the budget for simultaneous interpretation.

- **Whispering:** Here, the interpreter whispers translation to you when audience members make comments or raise questions. This approach works best if you are familiar enough with the language to understand most of what's said but need help here and there with specific words and phrases.

Once you've sorted out which kind you need, here's how to choose the right person and work effectively with her. If you can, allow up to a month to do the following:

- **Test your chemistry:** Some interpreters bring energy to the presentation; others can drain you. Spend time speaking with yours before you hire her. If you have time to interview a few candidates, all the better. You'll know someone's a good fit if she makes you laugh, for example, or calms you down. The interpreter shouldn't agitate you in any way—public speaking in a different culture is hard enough as it is. You should trust that she values your material and will represent it well.

- **Call in reinforcements:** If you can't find an excellent interpreter who's also a subject matter expert (a rare breed), use the professional interpreter as your primary source of translation—but also enlist an expert who speaks both languages to help out. That way you'll have someone who can correct the interpreter if she makes content mistakes here and there, in real time, or who can simply step in at a point where the material gets highly specialized or technical.

- **Prepare half as much material:** If you are given an hour, prepare 30 minutes' worth of material. It takes twice as long to convey your message with a consecutive interpreter—and even with the other types, you'll need extra time to translate any Q&A discussion.

- **Send your notes:** A week ahead of time, send over your notes or a transcript of a similar talk so the interpreter can practice. Even if you don't deliver your presentation exactly the same way, she'll get a feel for your material and style.

- **Work through idioms and metaphors:** Many phrases and sayings have no direct corollaries in other languages. If you've sent your notes or a transcript in advance, your interpreter will have time to flag anything that doesn't translate clearly. She can then suggest regional stories and meta-phors that would work in her culture.

- **Practice pacing:** Rehearse with your interpreter when you arrive to get a sense of how much mate-rial she can translate at a time. Have her coach you on your speed of delivery, so she can keep up *and* audience members can process what you're saying.

- **Complete each thought:** Each burst of content should be a concise but complete thought. Otherwise, you'll leave people hanging midphrase while the interpreter translates the first half of your point. Keeping your statements short and sweet makes it easy for the audience to follow you and engage with you.

Get the Most out of Your Q&A

A Q&A is a powerful, interactive way to address your audience's concerns *and* drive your point home. Always allow time for Q&A in a business presentation—trim your talk if necessary. When people leave the room with burning, unanswered questions, they won't adopt your ideas.

Get the most out of your Q&A by:

- **Planning when you'll take questions:** Establish early on if you want to field questions throughout your talk or save them until the end. If you need to build a thorough case, ask people at the very beginning to hold questions until the end. But if you're making a series of points, you can take questions after each one, while they're fresh in people's minds.

- **Anticipating questions:** You can spend hours preparing a presentation and deliver it beautifully— and then undo all your hard work and undermine your credibility by fumbling a response to an unexpected question. Think through *any* questions the audience might raise, from the mundane to the hostile. (See "Anticipate Resistance" in the Message section.) Prepare answers ahead of time so you won't be thrown off your game when all eyes are on you. Rehearse those answers, but still be mentally prepared for curveballs. Some questioners may feel a need to publicly challenge your idea. When that happens, it's important to keep your composure. Knowing your material inside-out will help immensely.

- **Listening empathetically for subtext:** Answer questions directly, but also try to identify and address any deeper ones behind them. (You'll often find a larger issue or unspoken motive lurking in the shadows.) Say you're in HR and you're hosting an orientation for employees from a recently acquired company. If people ask why they don't get to have monthly employee birthday parties anymore, you may be tempted to brush that off as silly—but the parties are probably a symbol of a bigger underlying problem. The question *behind* the question might be: "The culture we used to have isn't valued here. How can we hang on to some of the traditions that made our organization feel like a family?"

- **Admitting when you don't know something:** Don't fake an answer. Ever. Your audience will see right through it. If you don't know the answer to a question, say that—and offer to do some research after the presentation and get back to the group.

- **Keeping a tight rein on large or tough crowds:**
If you're presenting to a large group, ask a Q&A moderator to graciously take the microphone back after each question is asked. That way, one aggressive question won't turn into a barrage. Or, if you don't have a moderator, let the audience know up front that you're answering one question per person so more folks will have a chance to participate.

  When I took delivery training classes, I learned to acknowledge questions from angry inquisitors—but to look at *other* audience members when answering them so it's easier to move on to the next person and keep the discussion constructive. If your topic is emotionally charged or you're addressing a crisis—a safety recall, for example—have a facilitator filter the questions. He can compile a mix of tough questions and lighter ones that might get a laugh, and omit those that stray off topic or seem to have a personal agenda behind them. He can also plant questions the audience might be too intimidated to ask—for instance, "Will people lose their jobs if we don't make our numbers this year?"

- **Leaving a strong final impression:** Don't end abruptly after the Q&A—it feels incomplete and unsatisfying to the audience, and you'll miss an opportunity to reinforce your message. Wrap up the discussion with a brief summary that recaps the "new bliss" you're helping the audience achieve. (See "Make the Ending Powerful" in the Story section.)

Build Trust with a Remote Audience

Thanks to easily accessible webinar and teleconference technology, about 80% of corporate presentations are delivered remotely, according to several live surveys I've conducted with audiences at large companies in a range of industries. That's a stunning percentage. Any time technology revolutionizes how we communicate, there's a trade-off: Communication theorist Marshall McLuhan pointed it out when he proposed his system for examining the impact of new media on society. Use his system to examine remote presenting (figure 6-3), and you'll see both positive and negative outcomes.

Even though it's designed to connect people remotely and even globally, the technology isolates participants from human contact. So how do you solve that problem? How do you build trust with your remote audience? That depends on whether you incorporate video streaming.

With video streaming

When you're visible to the audience, your body language—particularly eye contact and gestures—can help

FIGURE 6-3

Pros and cons of remote presenting

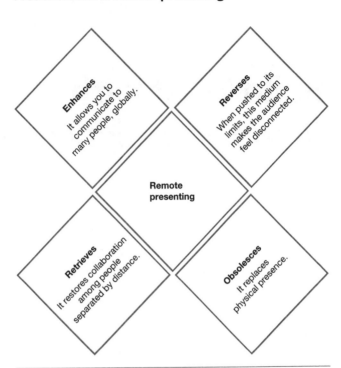

Enhances
It allows you to communicate to many people, globally.

Reverses
When pushed to its limits, this medium makes the audience feel disconnected.

Remote
presenting

Retrieves
It restores collaboration among people separated by distance.

Obsolesces
It replaces physical presence.

you connect with people (see "Communicate with Your Body" earlier in this section). If you glance at your notes or slides too often, your eyes will look shifty, so keep them trained on the camera as much as possible. Place the camera at eye level so you and the audience are on even ground. Looking down at it forces viewers to look up at you. Cinematographers use that trick to show a character's superiority—but the last thing you want to do is appear condescending.

If you can, deliver your presentation standing rather than seated. This allows you to move naturally—use your hands freely, lean forward, step back—which puts viewers at ease. Overall, make your movements expansive to connect with the people in the room. But when you want remote viewers to see certain gestures, keep those hand motions closer to your chest so they'll stay in the video frame. Use a high-quality video recorder and light yourself well: A professional-looking setup makes the audience feel valued.

Without video streaming

Your voice is your most valuable tool for building trust when the audience can't see you. But again, stand up—you'll sound more open and relaxed than if you're hunched over your computer. Hold people's attention by varying your volume, pitch, and tone (see "Keep Remote Listeners Interested" in this section). But don't overdo it—melodrama doesn't earn anyone's trust.

You can also build trust through the visuals you post. Create slides that convey an "open" feel by using type that's easy to read and keeping the graphics simple and clean. Also, in the spirit of transparency, let your audience download your deck.

Keep Remote Listeners Interested

When people tune in to a webinar or dial in to a teleconference, you can't see them, so their temptation to multitask is great.

My firm recently surveyed almost 400 people who've attended a webinar within the last year, and it turns out that more of them checked e-mail than doing any other activity—including *watching the webinar* (figure 6-4). That makes people's in-boxes your biggest competitor.

So what can you do to lure people away from their other tasks?

- **Break the content down into small bites:** Feed participants small, tasty morsels one by one so they stay tuned in. Move through your points quickly—don't spend a long time explaining concepts. And if you have slides, change them up about every 20 seconds.

FIGURE 6-4

E-mail is your biggest competitor

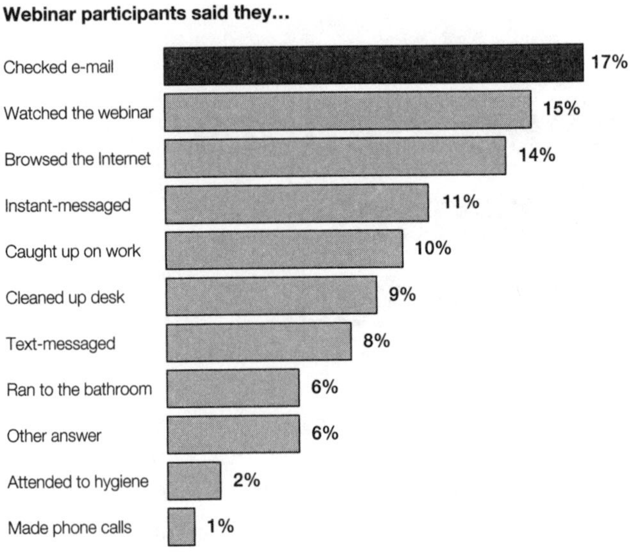

Webinar participants said they...

Checked e-mail	17%
Watched the webinar	15%
Browsed the Internet	14%
Instant-messaged	11%
Caught up on work	10%
Cleaned up desk	9%
Text-messaged	8%
Ran to the bathroom	6%
Other answer	6%
Attended to hygiene	2%
Made phone calls	1%

- **Make your presentation interactive:** Create useful activities for audience members to do, like spending a few minutes researching something and posting their findings in the chat window for everyone to see. If you ask people to take a survey, make sure the results will be of interest to them. And reward participants for paying close attention. When I was a guest on marketing consultant Chris Brogan's video blog, I placed a sign behind me that said, "First one who posts on Twitter that they saw this sign wins a free book."

- **Enjoy your own material:** Your enthusiasm needs to come through in your voice, especially if the audience can't see you on video. Smile as you share your material—and your voice will automatically take on a more cheerful tone. And if you say something funny, laugh a bit even if no one's in the room with you—it invites listeners to laugh, too.

- **Vary the voices:** Bring in other voices for interest. Try cohosting your presentation with another subject matter expert and bantering like morning show hosts. The audience will reengage each time a new speaker talks.

- **Pause strategically:** When audiences tune out remote presenters, the presentations sound like white noise to them. Sprinkle in pauses before points you really want people to hear. That'll cut through the white noise. When you begin speaking again, people will notice. Sometimes pausing also makes the audience think there's a problem with the technology—and people reengage to fiddle with their computers.

- **Picture your listeners:** Remember that you're talking to people, not machines. Picture their faces in your mind and imagine that you're having a live conversation with them. When I first started to present remotely, I struggled with talking naturally to the camera. So I took photos of my smiley staff members, cut out their faces, and taped them above my monitor (figure 6-5). This served as a visual reminder that I was speaking to real people.

FIGURE 6-5

Visualizing real people

Keep Your Remote Presentation Running Smoothly

Since remote audiences are so susceptible to distraction, even minor annoyances can derail your presentation. Keep things running smoothly with the following checklist:

- **Provide clear instructions:** When you send out an invitation explaining what the presentation is about, spell out how to register and log in, and explain any technical requirements up front so people don't sign up only to discover later that they don't have the equipment to participate.

- **Plan for technology snafus:** Give the audience contact information for technical questions. E-mail handouts ahead of time, and have slides in a handy location online just in case the webinar technology fails.

- **Test your slides:** Some webinar software "breaks" your slides by not properly displaying animations, builds, and transitions. Many path-based animations don't work or are so choppy they are ineffective. Color contrast can fade, and photos become pixilated. Test your slides on the exact same machine you're presenting from, because different operating systems and software behave differently. Click through each slide in the software and fix any problems.

- **Start on time:** Set up at least 30 minutes in advance to make sure your audio and video are working properly. You don't want attendees to think you're ill prepared as they listen to you fuss with technology issues.

- **Reduce personal noise:** Remove loud jewelry like bangle bracelets or earrings that can bang loudly against a headset. Minimize fidgeting. Don't drum your fingers, click pens, shuffle paper, or take sips of water near the microphone.

- **Reduce environmental noise:** Close your door and turn off fans and music. Close out of computer applications that have alert noises. Mute your microphone in the remote app when someone else is speaking so people won't hear your breathing or throat clearing. Turn off your cell phone, and put your office phone on the "Do Not Disturb" setting. If people are dialing in for a teleconference, don't put your phone on hold—they'll hear your hold music. Mute it.

- **Reduce visual noise:** Hide unnecessary software application windows and icons on your computer desktop to help focus the audience's attention. Use your mouse as a pointing device; don't frantically zing the arrow around your slides.

- **Reduce communal noise:** Remote listeners can hear just one person at a time, so don't have multiple conversations going at once during a teleconference. If someone in your room asks a question, repeat it so the remote audience can hear it.

- **Use a facilitator:** Relieve some of your pre-presentation stress by asking a facilitator to manage many of the details, like wrangling the technology, setting up the room, sending out the agenda and slides ahead of time, monitoring chat rooms, conducting surveys, and making sure people in all locations get a chance to be heard.

Section 7
Impact

We are competing for relevance.

—**Brian Solis,**
  principal analyst at Altimeter Group

Build Relationships Through Social Media

Social media channels give your audience a lot of control over your PR. People can broadcast bits of your content to their followers—quoting you, synthesizing your ideas, adding their own comments. Even if you have only 30 people in front of you when you speak, hundreds more—perhaps thousands, if your audience is highly networked—might catch a glimpse of what you're saying and what others think of it.

When the comments are positive, your ideas gain traction. At one event, a group of new attendees came to my talk about 15 minutes after I started. I found out afterward that an audience member had tweeted about my session, so some of his followers came to check it out.

But sometimes the comments aren't positive. Look at these sample tweets that went out during a higher-education conference presentation in Milwaukee:

@jrodgers
Starting to see the OMG I AM TRAPPED looks on faces.
#heweb09

@jShelK
We need a drinking game for every time he says "actually" and "actionable." #heweb09

@stomer
We need a tshirt, "I survived the keynote disaster of 09." #heweb09

Within hours, someone created a shirt on CafePress and shared it with conference attendees (figure 7-1).

FIGURE 7-1

CafePress T-shirt

In *The Backchannel,* communication consultant Cliff Atkinson writes about social media's impact on presentations. He points out that the "backchannel"—the stream of chatter before, during, and after your talk—is constructive when it:

- Enriches your message as people take notes, add commentary, and suggest additional resources on the topic

- Provides a valuable archive of information to review after the presentation

- Connects people in the room, building a community around the ideas

- Allows people who can't attend your live talk to follow dispatches and engage in conversations about it

- Increases your reach to more people

It's destructive when it:

- Distracts audience members so they pay more attention to the backchannel than to you

- Steers the conversation to unrelated topics

- Excludes audience members who are unaware of the backchannel or unable to join

- Limits people's ability to convey nuance or context, because of the brevity of the posts

- Injects a rude or snarky tone, since people feel comfortable tweeting thoughts they wouldn't say out loud

Your goal is to avoid a backchannel revolt, where people rally one another to reject your message. How? By making the folks online feel *heard*.

With or without your involvement, they'll have conversations about you. So participate. Engage with people like a skilled conversationalist, and they'll engage more fully and fairly with your ideas.

Build relationships with them by:

- **Observing their behavior:** Pay attention to what else they're commenting on. Active social media users can point you to hot spots online—a LinkedIn discussion group, for instance, or a brand's fan page—where you can begin or join conversations with potential customers or advocates.

- **Providing a channel:** Create a Twitter hashtag for your presentation and invite audience members to use it to chat with you and one another about your message. (Of course, this is appropriate only for external presentations with broad audiences. You wouldn't broadcast content from confidential company meetings, for example, or client sales calls.) Encourage attendees to use the backchannel before, during, and after your presentation; display your hashtag on an introductory slide.

- **Asking for their input:** Try presenting a partially developed idea and asking people to help you refine it through social media. I do this all the time and get useful replies. When I don't know much about an audience I'm preparing to address, I'll do some digging on my own—but I'll also ask my Twitter channel what might be on the minds of people attending a certain event, for instance, or working for a particular company or industry.

Spread Your Ideas with Social Media

Use social media content the way you use stories, visuals, and sound bites: to reinforce and spread your message.

You can write blog entries, post photos, commission infographics, and produce videos that enhance your ideas so your audience feels compelled to share them with others. If you want to get started but don't generate a lot of content yet, tweet links to other experts' articles and blog posts that support your talk.

Social media activity usually spikes during a presentation, with moderate chatter beforehand and afterward. Facilitate the conversation at its peak by:

- **Streaming your presentation:** Post a live video stream of your talk so people can attend remotely. This is the most direct way of extending your reach online, because the full message comes through, not just the chatter around it.

- **Time-releasing messages and slides:** Craft messages and slides expressly for social media channels, and use technology to automatically push them out at key moments during the presentation. You can download social media tools to program the time-release. Or you can add 140-character phrases to your notes field in PowerPoint and set them to auto-tweet when you advance the slides.

- **Selecting a moderator:** Assign someone—a colleague, a guest blogger, an audience member—to keep the social media thread constructive. Pick a person who's quick-witted, with a strong command of your material. Ask her to tweet key phrases as you say them, raise thought-provoking questions online, and bring the chatter back on topic when it starts to stray. Also have your moderator send out links to your slides (post them on slideshare.com or as pdfs on your website).

- **Repeating audience sentiment:** In addition to broadcasting your message, the moderator should repeat (and validate) what live audience members are saying. The currency of social media is reciprocity: If you don't spread the ideas of others, yours probably won't get anywhere.

- **Posting photos of your talk:** Enlist someone to photograph your presentation. To give social media users a sense of immediacy, he can work with your moderator to post the images while you're speaking.

- **Encouraging blogging:** Invite bloggers, journalists, and social media specialists to attend and cover your presentation. You'll increase your reach exponentially through their outlets and followers.

Social media guru Dan Zarrella studied what types of social media content people like to share during presentations. Here are a couple of tips from his research:

- **Don't be too overt:** People want to identify what's worth spreading on their own. So resist the temptation to use a little Twitter bird to flag sound bites you want the audience to spread. They'll actually get shared *less*.

- **Be novel:** Close to 30% of respondents in Zarrella's study said they were more likely to tweet or blog about a presentation if it was novel or newsworthy. For an idea to spread, it needs to be distinct and stand out.

After you present, post a video of your talk on your website and on LinkedIn, Facebook, and other social media sites. Though most backchannel activity typically happens during the talk, presentations sometimes go viral after the fact. (Great ones can get hundreds of thousands of views week after week.) Posting a video will also help you capture new audience members who didn't know about your presentation when you gave it or weren't able to tune in to the streamed version or the backchannel.

Gauge Whether You've Connected with People

Gathering feedback on your talk in real time and after you're done gives you different kinds of insights—all of them valuable.

Watch the backchannel

Have a moderator keep an eye on social media and send text messages to your cell phone if she thinks you should address any criticisms in a Q&A at the end of your talk. (She should pass along tough but fair comments—and filter out any chatter that would completely throw you off-kilter.) Or, if you're comfortable tweaking your message as you go, try putting your phone in silent mode, setting it on the podium or table in front of you, and glancing at it throughout the presentation. If the audience begins to revolt on the backchannel, you can change direction. Let people know you've monitored their sentiment because you want to address their concerns.

Watch the live audience

People in the room will show how they're feeling through their posture and facial expressions. Keep a keen eye out for physical cues that they're engaged in your material. One reason Steve Jobs could maintain a heightened sense of anticipation during a 90-minute keynote is because he had a gift for eliciting frequent physical reactions. In his 2007 iPhone launch presentation, the audience laughed 79 times and clapped 98 times—that's about one reaction every 30 seconds.

It's important to pick up on negative cues, too, so you can change course. Are audience members leaning back with their arms crossed? That could be a sign of resistance. Do they look tired? Are they fidgeting? Looking around? Checking e-mail? They may be bored or apathetic toward your ideas. If they're not demonstrating engagement by leaning forward, nodding, smiling, and taking notes, find a way of drawing them in.

One conference presenter could easily tell from body language that he was missing the mark with his audience—people clearly weren't into his message. Instead of dragging on, he stopped, admitted that he'd miscalculated when he'd prepared, and asked if he'd be given a chance to speak at the next conference if he promised to do a better job of understanding the group's needs. He got a standing ovation and an invitation to come back the next year.

Survey your audience

A survey isn't quite as immediate as backchannel chatter and other real-time feedback, but it gives you more control over the kinds of insights you'll get from the audience—and the comments may be more thoughtful. Make it short and direct, and have people fill it out on paper, online, or by e-mail. Explicitly ask them to be candid. Project a slide at the end of your talk encouraging people to rate you either right away, with their phones or tablets, or at their leisure.

Organizers of large events often survey audiences at all the sessions. If you're speaking at such an event, ask for the results. Even if you're doing a much smaller, less-formal presentation, you can ask one or two audience members whose opinion you value to give you an honest read on how it went. Tell them you're trying to refine your skills, and they'll probably be glad to help.

Analyze sentiment

If you're giving a high-stakes talk to a large group—a keynote address, for example—it's probably worth analyzing social media data, such as how many people blogged about your talk, how much traffic was driven to the press announcement through social media, and whether the coverage and comments were negative or positive. This will give you an even finer-grained picture of how well you've connected with your audience.

But the data can be daunting if you don't know what you're doing. Hire an analytics specialist to really dig in and help you see where you did well and where you can improve. In the analysis, you may discover a rival you didn't know about, for instance, or a new key influencer who drives buying behavior.

Analyze your reach

You can also use analytics tools to measure how many people spread your message through social media, how many clicked on the shared links, and whether your message was picked up by the people you'd want to hear it. Again, work with a data specialist.

It takes an iron gut to digest critical feedback. But it will make you a better presenter. Look closely at what the audience is saying about you, and modify your message, visuals, and delivery so you'll resonate more deeply with people in the future.

I launched my speaking career at a small annual conference. The first survey I got back said that I delivered a fire hose of valuable information, but the audience felt no connection. The event organizer told me I should incorporate more personal stories. It was painful to hear, but true. I took the feedback very seriously. In fact, it sent me on a several-year journey studying story principles and structure, which I now apply to presentations.

I'm not suggesting that every piece of feedback you get will be useful or even true. Usually, though, if you put the audience's needs first when you create your content and you're sincere in your approach when you deliver it, people will want to help you succeed.

Follow Up After Your Talk

Your presentation is done, and the adrenaline has stopped pumping. Now what?

Once you've won people over to your point of view, help them implement your ideas. Encourage them. Bring them new insights. Remove roadblocks. Keep your message alive by:

- **Sending personal notes:** It's rare to get a nice handwritten note these days, and people appreciate it when they do. Send a note whenever you feel grateful—to a colleague who helped you set up your presentation, for example, or to a busy executive who made time to attend and voice her support. (I've sent a few "I'm sorry" notes, too—it works both ways.) It can be a formal branded thank-you note or a clever card that touches on a personal conversation you had with an audience member. In a world of digital communications, a human touch stands out.

- **E-mailing the audience:** Follow up with an e-mail thanking people for their time. If appropriate, summarize your big idea, key points, call to action, and "new bliss." Many times, event organizers will share their attendees' e-mail addresses with you in lieu of paying speaking fees.

- **Being accessible:** If you presented within your organization, being accessible can mean hosting a lunch immediately after your talk, for instance, or blocking off your calendar so you can have an open door to answer questions in more detail. If you spoke to a broader audience and don't have people's contact information, send out thank-yous and other follow-up messages through blog and social media posts. Respond to anyone who starts a thoughtful conversation with you.

- **Sending materials:** If you promised the audience any materials in your talk, get them out right away. You might want to offer thank-you gifts such as free books or access to secure content, but check with the audience first. Many people have contracts with their employers that don't allow them to accept gifts from vendors or industry influencers.

- **Calling or meeting with individuals:** Suppose you presented a new initiative that's going to be demanding on your team. Spend time listening to each member's concerns. Pick up the phone if it's not possible to talk to everyone in person. Insights from these conversations can help shape your next piece of communication with the group. If you discover, for instance, that people are most worried about limited resources, describe your plans for shoring them up.

- **Booking "next steps" meetings:** Gather folks afterward to answer questions that require some research or analysis, and work together on a roadmap for achieving your goals. Facilitate collaboration in any way you can—for instance, order in lunch and ask your project leaders to brainstorm ways of marketing your initiative internally.

- **Presenting again:** Though your presentation is done, you may need to do a few more like it to share your message with other groups and move your ideas along. If you're selling a product or service, the purpose of the first presentation is usually to get a second presentation—that is, face-to-face time with a decision maker.

Think of each interaction as one moment in a larger relationship with your audience. That's the mind-set it takes to persuade people to change their thinking and behavior—and their world of work.

Index

Index

Index

About the Author

Communication expert Nancy Duarte has more than 20 years of experience working with global organizations and thought leaders from a wide range of industries and fields. Her company, Duarte, Inc., has created more than a quarter of a million presentations for its clients. Her team also teaches corporate and public workshops on writing and storyboarding effective presentations.

Duarte is the author of two award-winning books: *Resonate: Present Visual Stories That Transform Audiences,* which spent nearly a year on Amazon's top 100 business book bestsellers list; and *Slide:ology: The Art and Science of Creating Great Presentations.*

Duarte has been featured in *Fortune, Forbes, Fast Company, Wired,* the *Wall Street Journal,* the *New York Times,* and the *LA Times,* and on CNN.

Notes

Notes

Notes

Notes

Notes

Notes

Notes

Notes